Breaking the
Cycle of Offense

Larry Ollison, Ph.D.

Tulsa, Oklahoma

BREAKING THE CYCLE OF OFFENSE

Breaking the Cycle of Offense by Larry Ollison
Published by Insight Publishing Group & Larry Ollison
Ministries
8801 S. Yale, Suite 410
Tulsa, OK 74137
918-493-1718

Unless otherwise indicated, all scriptural quotations are from the New King James Version of the Bible ©1982 by Thomas Nelson, Inc. All Scriptures marked AMP are taken from The Amplified Bible ©1965, 1987; The Amplified Bible, Old Testament, Part One, ©1964; The Amplified Old Testament, Part Two, ©1962. The Amplified New Testament, ©1954, 1987 by the Lockman Foundation, La Habra, CA 90631.

ISBN: 1-930027-96-6

Library of Congress Card Catalog number: 2003102785

Printed in the United States of America

FOREWORD

God has given me the wonderful privilege of knowing men and women of God who walk in both wisdom and integrity. Larry Ollison is one of those men, and it has been a joy getting to know him.

Every believer who reads *Breaking the Cycle of Offense* will do himself a great favor! Living free from offense is one of the most important subjects that a Christian can master. Without an understanding of how and why Satan brings offense, you will be left defenseless. Living free from hurt and offense is one of the keys to experiencing the blessings of God in your life.

In this book, you will learn how Satan baits and traps people, the dangers of comparison, how to resolve issues, and how to live in "great peace."

Thank you, Larry, for sharing this important Bible truth with the Body of Christ in such a practical manner.

Vikki Burke

VIKKI BURKE, EDITOR

Vikki Burke is the wife and ministry partner of ICFM President, Dennis Burke. Together, they have affected thousands of people through a refreshing approach to God's work. They have ministered throughout the United States, as well as Australia, Asia, New Zealand, Canada, and the United Kingdom.

Compelled by the desire to see change in others, Vikki has delivered answers and insight to God's people. She herself is an author and her books include "Discover Relief and Refreshing," and the best selling book, "Aim Your Child Like an Arrow." Vikki has spoken at women's conferences, retreats, and marriage seminars. She has brought encouragement to many in the Body of Christ through the uncompromising Word of God.

ACKNOWLEDGMENTS

First of all I would like to thank my good friend and brother in the ministry, Col Stringer, for his teaching and inspiration. Col is a man of great character who walks in God's wisdom and understanding. Thank you, Col, for lighting the fire on the subject in this book.

I would like to thank Vikki Burke for the year of her life and the hundreds of hours spent editing and refining this book. Your talent and your great understanding of the Word formed this book into a magnificent manuscript. Countless lives will be changed, marriages saved, and lives restored because of your work.

Also, I would like to thank Alice McDermott for her oversight of this entire project. From conception to publication, her heart and her hands have touched every word. Thank you, Alice, for a job well done and for your loyalty to God's Word.

TABLE OF CONTENTS

Chapter One

Skandalon: Satan's Trap

O ffended people are everywhere—they're not only in the world, they are also in the church. No matter where you go in life, you can meet someone who is upset and offended. Even a routine trip to the grocery store can become a nightmare after a brief encounter with an angry checkout clerk and all you are thinking is: *Don't smash the eggs!* Because offense is such a widespread problem, Satan uses it as a tool to detour believers from what God has called them to do.

The Greek word used for offense in the New Testament is *skandalon* which can be translated "bait stick." The best way that I can communicate the purpose for a bait stick is to tell you about a program televised by the Discovery Channel demonstrating how the natives of one particular culture caught monkeys.

The natives placed a cage in the jungle containing a bait stick that the monkeys desperately wanted. As the monkeys approached the cage, they saw the bait inside and reached through the bars of the cage to grab it. However, as long as their fists were gripped around the bait stick, that they could not pull their hands out of the cage. Although the animals could have been set free from the trap, they desired the bait so badly, they refused to let go of the stick, making their seizure effortless for the locals.

When the natives approached with their clubs, the monkeys began jumping up and down and violently squealing, still unwilling to release the bait. They could have been set free at any time by simply letting go of the bait stick and pulling their hands from the cage, but they wouldn't. The closer the natives came to the animals, the more fierce their shrieking became. Fully aware that death was imminent, they stubbornly refused to loose the counterfeit treasure. The predators simply approached their target and clubbed them to death. The monkeys literally held life and death within their grasp.

That is a perfect illustration of what happens to someone who takes hold of offense. Whether you realize it or not, offense is Satan's bait stick that allows him to destroy your life. As long as you are determined to cling to the offense, your freedom will escape you in the same way it escaped the monkeys. While you desperately cling to the bait, the devil effortlessly moves in with death and destruction.

What is it that offends you? Is it as simple as somebody's breathing or the way they snort? Or is it what others say about you? Perhaps someone won't allow you to do what you want. Or possibly you're offended by something that was done to you as a child. Once the devil knows what offends you, he will continually send that particular thing into your life, hoping to lure you into his trap.

Sometimes harboring offense can feel good to your flesh because you are looking for the opportunity to get revenge. You know that you are seeking revenge when you mentally plot and scheme to get back at someone who has offended you. No longer seeking retribution is evidence that you have let go of offense.

However, as long as you cling to offense—like the monkeys held on to the bait stick—you can scream, you can jump up and down, you can even pray, but you will be snared by the devil's trap nonetheless. Even though offense and thoughts of revenge may feel good for awhile, they will soon bring ruin into your life.

All that was necessary for the monkeys to be set free was to let go of the bait. The only real thing that hindered them from freedom was their own intense desire. James 1:14 says, "Each one is tempted when he is drawn away by his own desires and enticed." In reality, the only thing that stood between complete freedom and ruin was the monkey's strong desire for the bait. A simple decision to let go brings life. In the exact same way, anyone willing to make the decision to release offense can live in complete freedom.

Peter Became an Offense to Jesus

When Jesus began to reveal to His disciples the things that He must suffer on the cross, Peter took Jesus aside and rebuked Him. In response to Peter's rebuke, Jesus said, "Get behind Me, Satan. You are an offense to Me, for you are not mindful of the things of God, but of the things of man" (Matthew 16:21-23).

This passage reveals several things to us. First, it illustrates that an offensive person is one who is more mindful of the things of men than of the things of God. Second, it tells us that while Peter's words were well-meaning, they were still offensive. It's important to realize that if Peter, who was a follower of Jesus, could be offensive, then so can those who follow Him today. Third, it demonstrates that despite Peter's offensive words, Jesus did not allow them to offend Him. What does this convey to you and me as Christians? It demonstrates that it is possible to be surrounded by people who are offensive, yet not allow them to get to you!

How could Jesus say, "You are an offense to Me" and yet not be offended? That sounds like a contradiction, but it simply means that although someone acts offensively toward you, it doesn't need to have an effect on you. However, you must realize that your struggle is not against flesh and blood. Ephesians 6:12 says, "For we do not wrestle against flesh and blood, but against principalities, against powers, against the rulers of the darkness of this age, against spiritual hosts of wickedness in the heavenly places." You can respond the way Jesus did toward Peter, by speaking directly to Satan. He said, "Get behind Me, Satan. I will not take your bait!"

The devil puts offense in your path, hoping you will grasp hold of it. If you do, he is waiting nearby to beat you over the head as hard as he can. All you have to do to be free is refuse to take hold of his bait.

You may think this sounds too simple, but one reason the things of God are misunderstood is because religious people have complicated the Word of God, making it difficult to follow. For instance, the Pharisees, who were the religious leaders of Jesus' day, added 2,000 man-made rules to the laws of God, which made them impossible for anyone to follow.

It is actually very easy to release offense and live in total peace and freedom. But the battle for freedom begins in your mind. Because you have the ability to control what you think, you can win every battle that Satan brings against you. Philippians 4:8 clearly teaches what believers are supposed to think about. It says,

> *Finally, brethren, whatever things are true, whatever things are noble, whatever things are just, whatever things are pure, whatever things are lovely, whatever things are of good report, if there is any virtue and if there is anything praiseworthy — meditate on these things.*

Although the Bible instructs you what to think about, it is still your choice to apply it. In addition to teaching you *what* to think about, it also empowers you to change the *way* you think. Romans 12:2 says, "Do not be conformed to this world, but be transformed by the renewing of your mind, that you may prove what is that good and acceptable and perfect will of God."

Begin your journey to freedom today by making this declaration out loud: "Because I refuse to be offended, I will not take hold of Satan's bait stick. Instead, I choose to forgive the offenses of others. I make the decision from this day forward to think on the things that are true, noble, just, pure, and lovely. As I study the Word of God, I believe my mind is being renewed."

This is the way you will stay free from offense!

Chapter Two

Blessed is He
Who is Not Offended

One of the most destructive, yet prevalent, issues that plagues the Christian community today is the vast number of people who are hurt and offended. As Christians, we must realize that offense is a very serious business. Make no mistake about it, the devil wants you to become hurt and offended in order to make you ineffective as a Christian—whether the offense you hold is against your spouse, your children, your neighbor, your family, or even against God.

Have you ever wondered why the devil is so determined to destroy God's people? Ezekiel 28:14 tells us that Lucifer (the devil) was at one time the anointed cherub—one who stood before God, leading heaven's hosts in worship. But after he tried to exercise his will over the Most High God, he was banished from heaven and was stripped of the anointing that he once possessed. Satan knows first-hand just how powerful the anointing is. And the fact that he no longer has access to the most powerful force in the universe—the burden-removing, yoke-destroying power of God—has made him hate God's people.

If that isn't enough, the anointing that Lucifer once possessed now dwells in the Body of Christ. First John 2:27 says, "But the anointing which you have received from Him abides in you." As a result of the anointing dwelling within Christians, the devil's mission to kill, steal, and destroy is focused against every born-again believer—including you and me!

Not only does the anointing abide in us, but we also have the Holy Spirit available to move *in* and *through* us. When a Christian is filled with the Holy Spirit, it means the Spirit of God sets up residence in our spirit, giving us the ability to walk in the anointing of the Spirit. Because we are God's creation, His handiwork, the devil will do anything possible to cause us to be ineffective in our Christian lives.

Remember, Satan has no new strategies—he uses the same old tactics to prevent Christians from producing fruit. And because offense prevents God from moving freely in your life, it has become one of Satan's most effective strategies. Whether you realize it or not, hurt and offense are designed specifically to prevent the Holy Spirit from bringing God's blessing to your life.

Offense Stops the Blessing of God

Jesus expressed the benefit of remaining unaffected by offense to His cousin, John the Baptist. While John was in prison, he sent his disciples to ask Jesus if He was the "Coming One" or if they should look for another.

Matthew 11:4-6 clarified the response Jesus sent to John the Baptist:

> *Go and tell John the things which you hear and see: The blind see and the lame walk; the lepers are cleansed and the deaf hear; the dead are raised up and the poor have the gospel preached to them. And blessed is he who is not offended because of Me.*

Some theologians actually believe by the way this passage is worded in the Greek that John the Baptist was offended at Jesus.

Notice the serious admonition that Jesus sent to John and his followers: "Blessed is he who is not offended because of Me." Jesus stressed that if John and his disciples would not become offended, the blessings of God would continue to flow to them. On the other hand, if they did become offended, then the blessings would be hindered.

You can be certain that the devil will send the opportunity to become offended your way, using any person or circumstance available. The critical question is: How will you react when offensive situations come? While one reaction will bring the anointing, the blessing, and the goodness of God, the other will bring a curse.

Although Galatians 3:13 says that Christ has redeemed us from the curse, *you* can make choices that will leave you vulnerable and defenseless to it. Through disobedience to God's Word, you can open a door to the devil that will allow him to take advantage of you.

For example, when you allow offense to consume your heart, it will begin to fester like a cancerous disease that will soon destroy you. Remember, even though the Word of God says offense will come, you can respond in the same manner in which Jesus did toward Peter and refuse to take hold of it!

Offense Comes with a Purpose

Like many carnal people, those who hold offense tend to defend themselves by saying, "I have a perfectly good reason for acting the way I do about this situation." But what they have failed to realize is that offense comes with a number of objectives. The devil will bring offense in order to destroy you, your anointing, your marriage, your family, your finances, and your friendships.

The second reason offense comes is to disrupt your communion with God. Mark 11:25 says, "And whenever you stand praying, if you have anything against anyone, forgive him, that your Father in heaven may also forgive you your trespasses." This verse clearly reveals the connection between forgiving others and being forgiven by God.

Offense will not only produce a barrier between you and God that hinders your prayer life, it will also keep you in a constant state of being upset towards the person who has offended you. Many times, the person with whom you are angry doesn't even realize that they have done something to hurt you. So, while you are being eaten up with hurt and unforgiveness, they remain carefree. However, the issue is not whether the hurt was intentional or not; what matters instead is that unforgiveness and offense are not allowed to take root in your life.

The third reason the devil brings offense into your life is to steal the Word of God that has been sown in your heart. Notice Mark 4:14-17 says,

> *The sower sows the word, and these are the ones by the wayside where the word is sown. When they hear, Satan immediately comes and takes away the word which was sown in their hearts. These, likewise, are the ones sown on stony ground, who when they hear the word immediately receive it with gladness. And they have no root in themselves, and so endure only for a time. Afterward when tribulation or persecution arises for the word's sake, immediately they stumble.*

After the Word of God has been sown in your heart, the devil will immediately bring trials, tribulations, and persecution for one purpose: to steal the Word of God before it takes root.

The Greek word *skandalizo* is not only translated "offend," but also "stumble." That means when someone is offended, there is a stumbling block in their path, prohibiting any advancement. Although these people receive the Word with gladness, they stumble when persecution or trials come, because they have no root in themselves.

Mark 6:2-3 records Jesus' teaching in Nazareth,

> *And when the Sabbath had come, He began to teach in the synagogue. And many hearing Him*

were astonished, saying, 'Where did this Man get these things? And what wisdom is this which is given to Him, that such mighty works are performed by His hands! Is this not the carpenter, the Son of Mary, and brother of James, Joses, Judas, and Simon? And are not His sisters here with us?' And they were offended at Him.

Verse 5 describes the result the residents of Nazareth experienced as a consequence of their offense toward Jesus: "Now He could do no mighty work there, except that He laid His hands on a few sick people and healed them." Notice, it does not say that Jesus *would not* do any mighty works there, it says He *could not*.

It is always God's desire to give good gifts to His children; however, offense can make the power of God ineffective. Matthew 7:11 says, "If you then, being evil, know how to give good gifts to your children, how much more will your Father who is in heaven give good things to those who ask Him!"

Don't allow offense to sidetrack you from the miracle God has planned for you! Instead, choose to forgive every hurt and wrongdoing so the stumbling blocks that are prohibiting your advancement in the Kingdom of God will be removed.

A Wrong Perception

Some people think they can simply receive deliverance from offense through prayer. But they fail to realize that after receiving prayer, *they* have both a choice and a responsibility to act on the Word of God. Again, according to Mark

4:15, once you have received prayer, the devil will come immediately to steal the Word of God from your heart. "...Satan comes immediately and takes away the word that was sown in their hearts."

Satan will tempt you to re-embrace the same old offense that once plagued you. He will build a case with thoughts such as: "You cannot just let go of the wrong that was done to you, or you will be nothing more than a door-mat. They need to pay for treating you so unkindly." Thoughts similar to these originate from Satan in hopes of reviving an old offense, but you must resist him. James 4:7 says, "Therefore submit to God. Resist the devil and he will flee from you."

Many people wrongly believe that being a Christian means that you are a wimp, and you are supposed to allow others to walk all over you, or use and abuse you. But that is simply not true. Jesus made a solemn statement concerning those who were responsible for offending others. He said, "Woe to the world because of offenses! For offenses must come, but woe to the man by whom the offense comes!" (Matthew 18:7).

However, not everyone is willing to do what it takes to be free from offense. Some people only want to be prayed for to receive a quick fix—a prayer that will solve all their problems and make them feel good again.

Don't get me wrong. I believe in the power of prayer. I know that the anointing of God is transferred by the laying on of hands, but you must be sure that you are not merely looking for a quick fix when seeking prayer. In other words, after receiving prayer, you must make the decision that regardless of how you feel, you are not going to be offended, and then you are going to take the responsibility to learn how to prevent future offense.

Four Motives for Leaving a Church

There are offended people everywhere—both in the world and the church. While some offended Christians continue to attend church, others become offended *at* the church and abandon it altogether. A recent survey taken at a ministers' conference revealed four basic reasons why people leave a church.

While the first 10-15 percent consisted of those who had passed away, the second group of 10-15 percent left a church because they either preferred a different style of music or wanted to be with friends. The third group of 10-15 percent left a church out of necessity, such as a job transfer. However, the fourth group consisted of an astonishing 60 percent—nearly two-thirds of those surveyed left a church because they were offended.

Seven Reasons for Offense

Although I have never personally conducted a formal survey, my studies have led me to the following seven basic reasons why people get offended:

1. **Oversensitive** - People who are overly sensitive are easily offended—making everyone nearby feel like they must walk on egg shells.

2. **Insensitive** - The next reason people become offended is exactly the opposite of the first reason—because

they are too insensitive, saying and doing things without thinking, they leave wounded people scattered along their path. This leads to rejection and offense.

3. **Unforgiveness** - Others are unwilling to forgive. Instead they cling to offenses. I know a person who held on to an offense for more than forty years, and it showed on their face.

4. **Unrealistic Expectations** - Another individual who is easily offended is one with a root of bitterness — falling victim to unrealistic or unfulfilled expectations.

5. **Rebellion** - Someone with a spirit of rebellion, who refuses to submit to any form of biblical correction or authority, can succumb to offense.

6. **Critical Spirit** - Still, others harbor a critical spirit — finding fault with everyone and everything.

7. **Feeling God is Unfair** - Finally, some are mad and offended at God — either disliking His plan or feeling He is unfair.

All of these people have so much pride that they don't truthfully see themselves. Only when they look at themselves honestly, the way God sees them, will they be diligent to keep their hearts clean from offense.

Chapter Three

The Dangers of Comparison

Another subtle trap that can put you on the road to offense is assuming or supposing something that you don't *know* for certain. This type of behavior is so dangerous because it is usually based on inaccurate information, particularly when it comes to God. In reality, there is no reason to suppose anything about God. You can know without a doubt what God will do because He has already stated it in His Word.

Religious people say, "You just never know what God is going to do." But the person making a statement like this either doesn't know or doesn't believe God's Word. The Word of God tells you exactly what He will do. God's will is clearly confirmed in His Word.

For instance, people have said, "If it's God's will, He will heal me." But that is simply a wasted statement because God has clearly stated throughout the Bible that it is His will to heal.

First Peter 2:24 says, "Who Himself (Jesus) bore our sins in His own body on the tree, that we, having died to sins, might live for righteousness by whose stripes you were healed."

Exodus 15:26 states, "For I am the Lord who heals you." Isaiah 57:19 says, "I create the fruit of the lips: peace, peace to him who is far off and to him who is near," says the Lord, "And I will heal him."

These and countless other Scriptures shed light on God's will concerning healing. Not only can you know that it is God's will to heal, but you can be confident that whatever God has said in His Word is available to *you*!

God always means exactly what He says. According to Hebrews 6:18, "It is impossible for God to lie." God has written His will in the Bible, and He will never change. Psalm 15:4 says, "He who swears to his own hurt and does not change." As a result, there is never an occasion to assume or suppose when it comes to the will of God.

The Kingdom of Heaven is Like a Landowner

Matthew 20:1-10 provides us with an excellent example of people who assumed they will receive something other than what they were told. It says,

> *For the kingdom of heaven is like a landowner, who went out early in the morning to hire laborers for his vineyard. Now when he had agreed with the laborers for a denarius a day, he sent them to his vineyard. And he went out about the third hour and saw others standing idle in the marketplace. And he said to them, 'You also go into the vineyard, and whatever is right, I will*

give you.' So they went. Again he went out about the sixth and the ninth hour and did likewise. And about the eleventh hour he went out and found others standing idle, and said to them, 'Why have you been standing here idle all day?' They said to him, 'Because no one hired us.' He said to them, 'You also go into the vineyard, and whatever is right, you will receive.' So when evening had come, the owner of the vineyard said to his steward, 'Call the laborers and give them their wages, beginning with the last to the first.' And when those came that were hired about the eleventh hour, they each received a denarius. But when the first came, they supposed that they would receive more, and they likewise received each a denarius. And when they had received it, they complained against the landowner.

Notice that those who were hired early in the morning agreed with the landowner to work for one denarius a day. But when the landowner hired more laborers that afternoon, they wrongly assumed they would receive more money than the newcomers. When they weren't paid any more for working longer hours, they were angry and complained to the landowner.

Complaining Will Get You Nowhere

Notice verse 12 says they complained, "saying...." Complaining always involves saying something. Do you remember what the Word says about the Hebrew children when they wandered in the wilderness? Whenever they felt the least amount of discomfort, they grumbled and complained. And when God heard their words, He was angry with them. (See Exodus 16.)

It may come as a shock to you, but God hears everything you say. There is nothing hidden from Him. You may successfully hide something from your husband, your wife, or your children. Perhaps you have even hidden something from the law, but nothing is hidden from God. Hebrews 4:13 says, "And there is no creature hidden from His sight, but all things are naked and open to the eyes of Him to whom we must give account."

Picking up at verse 11 from Matthew chapter 20, it says,

> *And when they had received it, they complained against the landowner, saying, 'These last men have only worked an hour, and you made them equal to us who have borne the burden of the heat of the day.'*

Notice that each man was hired to work a different number of hours, but all were paid the same. As a result, the laborers who worked all day complained even though they received exactly what they had agreed upon prior to working. A spirit of division and contention built among the workers.

Are You Angry Because I'm Generous?

The real problem arose when the laborers who were hired early in the day compared themselves to the others. If those who were hired late in the day had received a lesser wage, then they would not have had a reason to complain. But when they realized everyone received the same wage, regardless of the number of hours worked, they grumbled and complained. The equal treatment they were given made them angry. Let's continue with this parable, starting at verse 13,

> But he answered one of them and said, 'Friend, I am doing you no wrong. Did you not agree with me for a denarius? Take what is yours and go your way. I wish to give to this last man the same as you. Is it not lawful for me to do what I wish with my own things? Or is your eye evil because I'm good?'

In New Testament times, the phrase "evil eye" was a colloquialism, or idiom, of the day. In that day, when someone said you had an evil eye, they meant you were tight or stingy. Therefore, Jesus was speaking about the greed and stinginess of the workers who complained. What Jesus said carried this implication: "Are you angry because I'm generous?" Then He concluded with this astounding statement: "The last will be first, and the first last. For many are called, but few chosen."

The Dangers of Comparison

Because the real offense that arose among the laborers was caused by comparing themselves to one another, it will be profitable to study the dangers of comparison. Second Corinthians 10:12 says,

For we dare not class ourselves or compare our-
selves with those who commend themselves, but
they measuring themselves by themselves and
comparing themselves among themselves are not
wise.

Paul warned that comparing yourself with others would always get you into trouble. Have you ever wondered why the Apostle Paul said that comparison was unwise? It's because comparison is a type of pride. When you compare yourself to someone else, in essence, you are trying to find flaws or imperfections in the other person in order to feel superior to them—that is pride. Proverbs 16:18 warns, "Pride goes before destruction, and a haughty spirit before a fall."

When people make statements like, "Our church is the best church in town," it is nothing more than comparison and competition. What makes people think one church has to be better than another anyway? Why do people claim that one preacher is any better than another preacher? Acts 10:34 says, "In truth I perceive that God shows no partiality." One person is not better than another—they simply have different callings and when they fulfill their individual calling, it is expressed differently from anyone else.

The Word explicitly warns not to compare yourself with others, yet the Body of Christ is full of comparison and competition. Why would any Christian compete with another when God has offered the same promise to "whosoever"? It's because the one comparing and competing doesn't really believe that God will fulfill His promises for them. Perhaps they feel that God has abundantly blessed other people because He loves them more. But the truth is, God has more than enough to fulfill His promises for everyone!

You can have everything that God has promised in His Word! He has plenty, and just because He blesses another person with what you need, or desire, doesn't mean there isn't plenty more for you! He is El Shaddai, God Almighty, the source of all blessing.

Driving Out Comparison

You can drive out comparison and competition by becoming happy with what God has already given you. According to James 1:17, "Every good and every perfect gift comes down from the Father of lights, in whom there is no variation or shadow of turning." Who does God reserve these good and perfect gifts for? The gifts that James describes are for anyone who will believe and receive them — including you and me!

John 10:10 says, "...I have come that they may have life and that they may have it more abundantly." This verse is directed to believers. Accept what God has for you because everything He offers is good — He provides health, prosperity, favor, protection, and greater things than you can even imagine.

Paul expresses it this way in Ephesians 3:20: "Now to Him who is able to do exceedingly abundantly above all that we ask or think, according to the power that works in us." God has things planned for you that are greater than you can ask or think. Begin to stretch your imagination today and don't allow anything, such as offense or unforgiveness, to hold you back!

Chapter Four

Position is God-given

A carnal person judges worth by comparison, but as believers, we must begin to look at things from God's perspective. First Samuel 16:7 tells us exactly how God views things. It says, "For the Lord does not see as man sees; for man looks at the outward appearance, but the Lord looks at the heart."

The Apostle Paul, who warned us of the dangers of comparison, also clarifies how we ought to treat one another. Romans 12:16 says, "Be of the same mind toward one another, and do not set your mind on high things, but associate with the humble. Do not be wise in your own opinion."

In other words, Paul reminds us that our behavior ought to be equal toward everyone. Because Acts 10:34 tells us that God does not respect one person above another, He expects us to live the same way.

Furthermore, Romans 12:16 warns us not to become high-minded by lifting ourselves up into a wrong position. Attitude toward position is a problem that hinders far too many people in the Body of Christ. All too often, people seek a place of position or some other means to get recognition.

Position is God-given

Position in God's kingdom is determined by God, not by man. Ephesians 4:11 says, "And He Himself gave some to be apostles, some prophets, some evangelists, and some pastors and teachers." Although God has called some into fivefold ministry, He has given everyone the ministry of reconciliation no matter where they are employed. Second Corinthians 5:18 says, "Now all things are of God, who has reconciled us to Himself through Jesus Christ, and has given us the ministry of reconciliation."

Although I have several doctors in my church, I was impressed when they introduced themselves by their first name, instead of doctor so-and-so. Not only does a doctor have a prominent position, but also an impressive degree. So why didn't the doctors in my church flaunt their position by using their formal title in their introduction? They didn't need to use a professional title to identify themselves because they are confident in who they are as a person. Their position or degree isn't who they are; it simply enables them to fulfill their calling.

The Desire for Greater Recognition

Many churches find themselves in a constant struggle with people seeking a position, or other forms of recognition, out of a wrong motive. Some church members actually feel that because they have been at the church from the beginning, they deserve more than a newcomer. What privileges do they feel they deserve? Some want a prominent seat, while others want a position as elder or deacon.

Again, the attitude that exalts one person above another is rooted in nothing more than pride and fear. Some become fearful that another person is going to take their place, and they won't be considered important anymore. They haven't realized that there are enough seats at God's table for everyone. No one has to be kicked out of their seat in order to make room at God's banquet table.

I have been around ministers who introduce themselves as "Pastor." Even their wives refer to them as "Pastor," as though it were their first name. But, how would it look to a pastor if a prophet of God introduced himself as "Prophet?" What about an evangelist? Everyone would think that sounded pretty ridiculous, wouldn't they?

There is no need to insist upon being addressed by a particular title. Insisting that others use a title when speaking to you only serves to make you look more important in your own eyes. In fact, many times the need to flaunt your position is characteristic of insecurity.

Why do you suppose a minister really wants to know how many people are in my church? Only my close friends are really interested in how my church is doing. There is usually only one reason a minister asks how many people are attending my church—so he can categorize me.

If I say that we have 500 people, then he knows how to judge me in comparison to himself. If he has 200 people, then he judges me better then himself. However, if he has 1,000 people, then he judges me as less. This is exactly what Paul warned about! Comparing yourselves among yourselves is dangerous business! (2 Corinthians 10:12)

Let's look at another common situation in church in which comparison takes place. Suppose there is a man who lived his entire life drinking and selling drugs. Then, as an elderly man, he gets saved and his entire life turns around. I could compare myself to him by complaining, "It's not fair that I have lived a good Christian life from my youth, but the guy who accepted the Lord late in life gets the same reward. Until a few days ago, he lived a disgraceful existence; he shouldn't get the same reward that I get."

A person who thinks like this doesn't realize that when you step over into eternal life, salvation is equal with everyone. In other words, the person who was saved for 60 years will receive the exact same salvation as the person who was saved on their deathbed. Both accepted the sacrifice of Jesus. Now they are both forgiven and righteous in God's eyes.

Although it may not seem fair by man's standards, according to God's standard, it is just. God is not required to be fair in the way man judges fairness. He is, however, just! Psalm 97:2 says, "Righteousness and justice are the foundation of His throne." God has decided to be generous to anyone who gives their life over to Him, even if they do so with their last breath.

Remember the parable in which the landowner paid one laborer a denarius to work all day and he paid another laborer one denarius for working part time. Because they both received what they had agreed upon, it is considered just in God's sight.

The person who still says this is unfair is thinking like a carnal man. Jesus rebuked Peter for thinking that way. He said, "You are an offense to Me, for you are not mindful of the things of God, but the things of men" (Matthew 16:23).

Comparison Involves Pride

Paul warned us not to compare ourselves with one another because comparison involves pride. Then, in speaking to his spiritual son, Timothy, Paul says,

> *Command those who are rich in this present age not to be haughty, high-minded, nor to trust in uncertain riches, but in the living God who gives us all things richly to enjoy.*
>
> *1 Timothy 6:17*

Paul cautioned Timothy about becoming high-minded and trusting in riches. Instead, he exhorted him to think soberly about himself, trusting in God alone. When anyone begins to think that a position of prominence is owed to them because they have worked harder or longer, they are exalting themselves above others—which is what this Scripture warns against.

For example, my wife and I attended a ministers' conference where a very well-known minister walked up to the front of the church, looking for a chair reserved with his name on it. When he didn't find it, he asked to speak with the head usher. After they had finished talking, the minister turned and left the meeting—apparently there wasn't a seat reserved for him. Regardless of how many television stations you are on, the church doesn't need strife, contention, and pride sitting on the front row.

High-mindedness is Pride

The word *pride* simply means high-mindedness. In other words, a high-minded person has a higher opinion of themselves than they ought to. Even if someone is greatly talented, is an outstanding vocalist, excellent on the keyboard, or an exceptional administrator, it doesn't mean that they have arrived at a place where they no longer need to hear the Word of God. Just because someone does a good job doesn't mean that they are better than someone else. Considering yourself better than someone else, for any reason, is high-mindedness.

Pride, envy, and offense are the kiss of death for any church that will allow it inside their congregation. Long-standing church members who think that they should have greater privileges are demonstrating pride. Just because you have been in a church from the beginning doesn't mean that you can run the church. These people exalt themselves into a dangerous place, and they can literally stifle the growth of the church by excluding people.

What many people don't understand is that there are good reasons for reserving seats. For instance, a seat might be reserved for the person who displays the overhead projector during a worship service. Other seats might be reserved for a person the pastor may need during the meeting, like a worship leader. Ushers usually have a reserved seat on the aisle so they can get up without disturbing those around them.

However, something is drastically wrong with the motives of a person whose goal is to be an usher in order to get a better seat. The person who thinks that way is operating in envy, strife, and contention. They come to destroy the work of God. That's why many churches reach a membership of around 250, level off, and then never grow anymore. God cannot work in a church where people have bad motives.

If you really want to do all you can for God and you feel that God is calling you to move to a higher level of living, then petty issues must be pushed aside to allow the people who are coming in at the eleventh hour to do what God has called them to do. Remember, God's kingdom is not based on seniority.

Chapter Five

Harder to Win Than a City

As a believer, you know that Jesus bought your freedom with the price of His blood—you are free to do whatever He asks of you. Speaking to believers, the Apostle Paul says in Galatians 5:1, "Stand fast therefore in the liberty by which Christ has made us free, and do not be entangled again with a yoke of bondage."

In other words, because Jesus paid such a precious price to make you totally free, you should do whatever it takes to avoid becoming ensnared again. Jesus died to liberate you from all fear, sickness, poverty, depression, and every other form of bondage that the devil tries to burden you with.

You are free to either go where God tells you to go, or remain inactive when He tells you to wait. No matter what He directs you to do, nothing should hinder you. Regretfully, there are many things that have kept Christians in bondage even though Jesus paid an awesome price for their freedom.

Proverbs 18:19 says, "A brother offended is harder to win than a strong city: and contentions are like the bars of a castle." There are two things this verse identifies that every Christian must avoid—contention and offense. Let's study the latter portion of this verse first. Notice that it says, "Contentions are like the bars of a castle." Bars do two things. First, they prevent people from getting out. Second, they prevent people from getting in.

This verse emphasizes that contention—strife, quarrels, and disputes—creates prison bars or barriers in your life. Your involvement in any form of contention will hinder you from either getting to the place you should be or getting out of the situation that has ensnared you.

Now let's study the first part of Proverbs 18:19. It says, "A brother offended is harder to win than a strong city." Have you ever had a desire to minister to a particular person but sensed, that no matter how carefully you phrased it, they would get offended? Most likely, we have all been in a similar situation. It is very sad to have a friend or acquaintance with whom you can't be open and truthful because you're so concerned about how they will react.

Offended people live stirred-up, angry, and agitated, with a ready-to-bust attitude. Everyone around them feels that they must walk on eggshells—fearful that at any moment they might say the wrong thing. How many times have you thought, *I believe the Lord has given me something to tell that person, but I wonder how they will react?* If you are like me, you have thought that many times. In reality, when we wonder how someone will react to what we say, we are really wondering if they will become offended as a result of our conversation.

Have you ever heard someone say, "I would tell them, but I don't think it would settle well"? What do you suppose is meant by that statement? It means that the person they want to speak with is wound up tight, agitated, and ready to snap at any moment. You're concerned that if you say anything, it will be the very thing that makes them snap or explode. They might snarl at you with a retort like: "How dare you talk to me that way! What exactly do you mean by that remark?" And since we have all been in that awkward situation at one time or another, we've become reluctant to offer our counsel ever again.

Let Offense Roll Off Your Back

Jesus made a statement regarding the poor in Matthew 26 that we can parallel with an attitude of offense. When the disciples questioned the woman for pouring expensive perfume on Jesus' feet, they said, "Why this waste? For this fragrant oil might have been sold for much and given to the poor" (v. 8-9). Do you really suppose the disciples had a legitimate concern for the poor? I don't think so. They were more concerned about the profit they could have made from selling the perfume.

But notice how Jesus answered them: "For you have the poor with you always, but Me you do not have always" (v. 11). What exactly did Jesus mean by this statement? Was He indicating that He had created a certain number of poor people to balance out society? No, that's not what He meant. Instead, He meant that there would always be an element of society that would not accept Him as their Lord. Even a fragment of those who did accept Him would not walk in the fullness of their inheritance.

There will always be a certain group of people who will not live in prosperity because they think it's wrong. And there will be some who won't receive divine healing because they either don't believe healing is for everyone, or they believe divine healing passed away with the apostles. Jesus could just as easily have said, "Not only will we always have the poor with us, but also the sick, the lost, the defeated, and the depressed."

Just because there are Christians who suffer doesn't mean that it is God's will. Second Peter 3:9 makes that very clear:

> *The Lord is not slack concerning His promise, as some count slackness, but is longsuffering toward us, not willing that any should perish but that all should come to repentance.*

It's not God's will that anyone should perish, be poor, be sick, or be offended. However, there will always be those people who miss the perfect will of God.

Jesus was not making a bad confession when He said, "Offenses must come" (Matthew 18:7). No, He was stating a fact. Jesus was simply making the point that as long as you are in the world, you will be surrounded by offensive situations; however, you don't have to become offended by them. Whether you believe it or not, you can, as a born-again believer, let offensive words roll off your back like water rolls off a duck's back. You do not have to become offended!

Controlling How You React

Although you cannot control how people act, you can control how *you* react. In fact, when offensive situations arise, they can become your opportunity to shine! You can literally make the decision that regardless of the way others act, you will not allow them to offend you. Furthermore, you can be surrounded by an atmosphere of strife and contention and be the only person who remains totally free from their influence.

You have probably worked in an environment where everyone in the office, in the field, or in management was mad most of the time. Perhaps you have worked at a company where people said cruel things to one another, obviously disliking each other. Maybe you innocently asked someone to help you, and they refused.

By the power of the Spirit of God, you can endure in any type of unpleasant environment and yet remain undisturbed by it. It's even possible to be surrounded by rude or hateful people and still maintain your joy. You might think that's impossible, but it isn't. However, to live free from the influence of the world, you must do something. You must make a decision. If you want to live free from the circumstances around you, you must decide that you are not going to become offended.

I am by no means suggesting that you are supposed to pretend that offense or hurtful words don't exist. That's only denial. And the old adage, "Sticks and stones may break my bones, but words will never hurt me," is not true. Words do have the power not only to hurt but also to destroy. Proverbs 18:21 says, "Death and life are in the power of the tongue, and those who love it will eat its fruit." However, anyone who refuses to receive hurtful, destructive words cannot be harmed by them.

Ephesians 4:26 says, "Be angry, and do not sin. Do not let the sun go down on your wrath, nor give place to the devil." Is it actually possible to be angry and not sin? Yes, if you get angry but refuse to react. Then again, this verse says that if you do get angry without resolving it before you go to bed, you have sinned.

Ask the Holy Spirit today to help you be unaffected by the offensive ways of others. Don't be among those who refuse to control their reactions. Instead, draw on self-control, one part of the fruit of the Spirit.

Chapter Six

Resolving Offense

In order to resolve an offense, according to Matthew 18:15-17, you must go to the person who has hurt or offended you and work it out. Notice what it says,

> Moreover if your brother sins against you, go and tell him his fault between you and him alone. If he hears you, you have gained your brother. But if he will not hear, take with you one or two more, that by the mouth of two or three witnesses every word may be established. And if he refuses to hear them, tell it to the church.

According to this Scripture, if the other party refuses to work through the problem, then you are supposed to take someone with you to attempt to settle the issue. And if they still refuse to cooperate, then you are free from your scriptural duty, and you can walk away from the situation without any further responsibility. However, if you still desire a relationship with that person, then you can take it before the church. If the person rejects this last attempt to resolve the problem, then there is simply nothing further that you can do except keep your heart pure.

It is impossible to build relationships that are founded on contention, strife, envy, and pride without the devil gaining an entrance into your life through them. Proverbs 13:20 says, "He who walks with wise men will be wise, but the companion of fools will be destroyed." That's why you must choose your friends very carefully, and then remain diligent to guard those associations.

Galatians 5:15-16 further bears out this point when it says, "But if you bite and devour one another, beware, lest you be consumed by one another. I say then, walk in the Spirit and you shall not fulfill the lusts of the flesh." You choose to walk in the Spirit by faith. When you walk by faith, you cease to walk in fear. As long as you continue to walk by faith, you won't give place to the flesh. In other words, you are not building a foundation in your life from which the devil can control you.

The Little Foxes That Steal

Most of the time people get offended over petty issues. Song of Solomon 2:15 states that it is "...the little foxes that spoil the vines." As hard as it is to believe, churches have actually been split over petty issues like the color of the carpet or the type of hymnals to purchase. People can get offended over such trivial issues that hold absolutely no significance to the overall scope of life. It's time that the Body of Christ grows up and stops allowing unimportant matters to hurt and offend them. Think about it. You could be spending your time growing in the Word of God, instead of arguing over the color of the choir robes or the placement of the flag.

Letting Go of Offense

Some time ago, I conducted a wedding rehearsal where the mothers of the bride and groom got into a fist-fight over where I was supposed to stand. They had both been holding their grandbabies, then suddenly handed them over to somebody else and squared off. They ended up on the floor, poking each other in the face. And in my infinite wisdom, I let them fight it out until they were done.

The next day, at the wedding, was just as pitiful. Although both mothers acted like nothing had happened, the woman who sang at the ceremony forgot the words to the second verse and threw down the microphone saying, "Forget it!"

Is it any wonder why people are sick, in financial trouble, or have problems with family? Could it be possible that offense is preventing the blessing of God?

I knew one man who was continually offended at his wife. He refused to release the offense because many of his conversations revolved around her and how bad she treated him. He would even get mad at her when she treated him nice because it didn't give him anything to complain about. There are actually people who feel that they would lose their identity if they released their offense. They have become so accustomed to their life centering around a wrongdoing that if they let it go, then they wouldn't have anything to talk about. But do you remember what Philippians 4:8 says?

*Finally, brethren, whatever things are true, what-
ever things are noble, whatever things are just,
whatever things are pure, whatever things are
lovely, whatever things are of good report, if
there's any virtue and if there's anything praise-
worthy — meditate on these things.*

The Greek word for *meditate* in this verse means,
"to mutter softly over your lips." Therefore, according to
this verse, not only are you to think about good things but
also mutter good things. So you must quit thinking and
speaking about offense and the things that push your buttons. Refuse to talk about what makes you angry because
doing so is in direct disobedience and rebellion to the
Word of God.

First Samuel 15:23 clearly states, "For rebellion is
as the sin of witchcraft, and stubbornness is as iniquity
and idolatry." Disobedience and rebellion toward God
each give place to other sins. When you are offended and
you refuse to let it go, you are simply being rebellious and
stubborn.

I have heard people say, "I know I'm not supposed
to say this and I should forgive this person, but let me tell
you what happened." By the very words spoken from
their own mouth they admit: "I know the Word of God
says I shouldn't be saying or thinking this, but it feels so
good that I'm going to do it anyway." Consequently, they
have chosen to live by their feelings instead of living by
faith in God's Word. However, in order to grow and
increase in life, you must obey the Word of God in spite
of your feelings.

Grace to Do the Impossible

You may be wondering if it is possible to live by faith and not your feelings. Yes, it is possible. You can do so by the grace of God that enables you to do the impossible. Hebrews 12:15 says, "Looking carefully, lest anyone fall short of the grace of God, lest any root of bitterness springing up cause trouble and by this many become defiled."

Grace is available to anyone who will partake of it. However, whenever you fall short of God's grace, a root of bitterness can take hold which, according to this verse, will cause a tremendous amount of trouble. And despite what some might think, it doesn't just cause trouble for the person who is bitter. Instead, it causes trouble for everyone around them as well. Notice that the Word says, "...many become defiled."

Most of the time, people with a root of bitterness don't recognize it in themselves. It's like the person who has bad breath or body odor in a room full of people. Although they smell really bad, they don't know it. A root of bitterness can be seen by others, but not always by the one who is defiled by it. Many times these same people wonder why they don't have friends, but all that comes out of their mouth is gossip, revenge, envy, and strife.

Some people think they can pray and ask God to take the offense from their heart, but it won't help. God has given you the authority to resist temptation and sin. James 4:7 says, "Therefore submit to God. Resist the devil and he will flee from you." So when someone says they can't help being angry and bitter, they are not telling the truth. God's Word says *you* resist the devil and he *will* flee.

Furthermore, 1 Corinthians 10:13 says, "No temptation has overtaken you except such as is common to man; but God is faithful, who will not allow you to be tempted beyond what you are able, but with the temptation will also make the way of escape, that you may be able to bear it." There is no temptation that you are unable to overcome by the power of the grace of God. Anyone who says they can't help being offended is deceiving themselves. The truth is that God has given His grace, His Word, His power, and His ability to do the impossible. In other words, God has given *you* the power to do everything that is written in His Word — including resisting hurt and offense.

Be a Doer, Not a Hearer Only

There are people who use the excuse that they are working at overcoming offense. But that's not what the Bible instructs us to do. James 1:23-25 clearly states that only the doers of the Word will be blessed.

> *For if anyone is a hearer of the word and not a doer, he is like a man observing his natural face in a mirror; for he observes himself, goes away, and immediately forgets what kind of man he was. But he who looks into the perfect law of liberty and continues in it, and is not a forgetful hearer but a doer of the work, this one will be blessed in what he does.*

A doer of the Word is not someone who merely listens to what the Word says, but rather applies what he has heard to his life. How do you suppose it would sound if someone said, "I am working at not lying"? No, if you simply tell the truth, you won't lie! It's not those who are working at not lying who are blessed, but those who speak the truth.

God doesn't accept the idea of "working on it" any more than you would if your spouse said he or she was "working on" being married. Your spouse would get the slack jerked out of him or her very quickly!

When someone states that they are "working on it," what they are actually revealing is that they are not yet willing to obey God. Isn't that right? It's a whole lot easier to justify yourself by saying that you are working on something than it is to implement the Word of God or to admit you're in sin. Many times you can con people with such statements, but you can't con God because He looks upon the heart.

There is not one sin that the blood of Jesus cannot eradicate. His blood is all-powerful. And as a result, there is no excuse for a Christian to be offended. No one—no matter how heartbreaking, horrific, or desperate the situation—can develop an excuse for being offended that is acceptable to God.

You may have convinced yourself that your basis for offense is a worthy one, but you will never persuade God. He gave His Son to die so that all of humanity could be forgiven of their shortcomings. If you have accepted God's forgiveness, then you must be willing to give it to others. "For if you forgive men their trespasses, your heavenly Father will also forgive you" (Matthew 6:14).

There is no permissible excuse for disobeying God. When you stand before Him, and He asks, "Why didn't you obey My Word?" you cannot come up with an excuse that will satisfy God. You may offer an excuse, but He will reply, "I empowered you with supernatural ability to do all that was written in My Word. All you had to do was make the decision to obey." And the bottom line will be that you simply made poor choices.

In the same manner, there is no acceptable excuse for harboring unforgiveness because of an offense. Although someone always tries to defend *their* reason for being offended by saying, "But you don't know what they did to me, or how many years I have had to put up with it." However, the Lord didn't exclude anyone when He said, "Whenever you stand praying, if you have anything against anyone, forgive him, that your Father in heaven may also forgive you your trespasses" (Mark 11:25). So, apparently it doesn't matter what the offense was, you are still required to forgive.

Don't Subject Yourself to Abuse

At this point, I want to dispel a very common misconception about abuse and offense. Contrary to what most people think, removing yourself from an abusive situation doesn't necessarily mean you are offended or unforgiving.

For example, if your husband beats you, God does not expect you, or your children, to remain in such an environment. And leaving such a horrendous situation does not necessarily mean that you are offended. It is actually possible to leave an abusive situation and not harbor offense toward the abuser.

However, if you leave that situation with hatred or bitterness towards your abuser, then you are in direct disobedience to God's Word. Jesus did not harbor hatred or bitterness toward those who betrayed Him or nailed Him to the cross. Instead He said, "Father, forgive them, for they do not know what they do" (Luke 23:34). Jesus demonstrated His love for the Father by obeying His commandments. First John 5:2-3 says,

> *By this we know that we love the children of God, when we love God and keep His commandments. For this is the love of God, that we keep His commandments. And His commandments are not burdensome.*

Do you love God? How do you demonstrate your love for God? According to this verse, crying, praying, or even tithing doesn't prove your love. Instead, your love is proven only when you keep His commandments.

When the Lord said in Matthew 19:19, "Love your neighbor...." He didn't mean to love only those who love you in return. His commandment to love is without exception.

Choose to prove your love for God by obeying His Word. He has given you the anointing, the grace, and the power to love and live free from offense.

Chapter Seven

Escaping the Snare of the Devil

Satan's greatest fear is that the Body of Christ will discover the principles that will enable them to escape his snares. Once they do, he will lose his ability to entrap them. Second Timothy 2:25-26 reveals a three step principle that will help you avoid the devil's snare. It says,

> *In humility correcting those who are in opposition, if God perhaps will grant them repentance, so that they may know the truth, and that they may come to their senses and escape the snare of the devil, having been taken captive by him to do his will.*

The first step that is revealed in escaping the snare of the devil is to "know the truth." You may be thinking, *But how do I know what is truth?* Jesus Himself answers that question in John 8:31-32, "If you abide in My word, you are My disciples indeed. You will know the truth, and the truth will set you free." In other words, the Word of God is truth. John 17:17 bears this out. It says, "Your word is truth."

Furthermore James 4:7 says, "Therefore submit to God. Resist the devil and he will flee from you." How do you submit to God? By obeying His Word and by knowing the truth.

As an exhortation to praise God, the psalmist said, "For the word of the Lord is right, and all His work is done in truth" (Psalm 33:4). God's Word and His works are on a collision course. In other words, when His Word is obeyed, His works will result.

Numbers 23:19 further declares, "God is not a man, that He should lie, nor a son of man, that He should repent. Has He said, and will He not do? Or has He spoken, and will He not make it good?" When you obey the Word of God, He will perform what He promises and nothing less. The works of God are a direct result of His Word.

Come to Your Senses

The second step revealed in this verse is to "come to your senses." Coming to your senses simply means that you snap out of the stupor that you have been living in. Have you ever seen someone in a stupor suddenly snap out of it? Perhaps you have experienced it personally.

God calls His people to awaken from their stupor in Isaiah 60:1. He said, "Arise, shine; for your light has come! And the glory of the Lord is risen upon you." Those who remain in a state of slumber will undoubtedly become ensnared by the enemy.

In Ephesians 5:14, the Apostle Paul's cry is to awaken believers: "Awake, you who sleep, arise from the dead, and Christ will give you light." Once again, the call of God to awaken believers out of their stupor is so that the light of Christ will shine upon them.

Escaping the Snare

And finally, the result of knowing the truth and coming to your senses is "escaping the snare of the devil." How badly do you want to be set free? How desperate are you to escape future snares of the devil? Only when you saturate yourself in the Word of God and snap out of your stupor will you avoid the devil's snare.

Say this out loud: "I know the truth and have come to my senses; therefore, I will escape the snare of the devil." Too many people are trying to get set free in some other way, but if there was another way Jesus would have used it. Instead, every time the devil attempted to ensnare Jesus, He drove him away by speaking the truth—God's Word. Notice Jesus' response when the devil tempted Him in the wilderness. Matthew 4:3-4 says,

> *Now when the tempter came to Him, he said, 'If You are the Son of God, command that these stones become bread.' But He answered and said, 'It is written, Man shall not live by bread alone, but by every word that proceeds from the mouth of God.'*

Jesus repeated this process of speaking the truth three times before the devil left. The Word of God—the truth—must be applied before freedom is experienced. Although the method may sound simple, don't miss the blessing of God because truth appears to be simplistic.

Chapter Eight

Unforgiveness is a Choice

"Unforgiveness" is a word that can be used inter-changeably with the word "offense." You cannot be in a state of offense and forgiveness at the same time—they have conflicting results.

You can claim whatever you like, but if you refuse to forgive someone, it's because you have not chosen to do so. It's very likely that the person you need to forgive has acted like somewhat of a jerk, but regardless of the way he has acted, you don't have to allow him to offend you. You can release the hurt, the pain, and the offense and walk away completely free from it.

Although you cannot stop people from being offen-sive, you can prevent them from offending you. You shouldn't concern yourself with what others do; instead, just focus on yourself. If others choose to be offended, don't let it become a stumbling block for you. Offense will affect you physically, spiritually, and financially. It will even affect your job performance and the atmosphere of your home. Offense will affect every aspect of your life, so the success of your life depends upon it.

Don't Be a Stumbling Block

Romans 14:21 says, "It is good neither to eat meat nor to drink wine, nor to do anything by which your brother stumbles or is offended or is made weak."

You may feel that you can do whatever you desire, and it's no one's business. If they don't like it, then it's just too bad. That is exactly the attitude that the devil can use to cause others to become offended and fall. You don't want to be used by the devil, do you? Then adopt the attitude that cares how your behavior affects others, and it will not result in causing another person to stumble.

For instance, some Christians think there is nothing wrong with drinking a beer with a pizza, or having wine with dinner. Although some denominations may teach that drinking a beer with your pizza will send you to hell, it won't. However, even though it may not send you to hell, it may cause a brother or sister to stumble and become offended.

Do you realize that people are watching you? You are to live in a manner that becomes an example to others. Second Corinthians 3:2 says, "You are our epistle written in our hearts, known and read by all men." If you do something that causes others to stumble, then Satan has used you to position them for offense.

Personally, I would never do anything that caused others to be led astray because I love them too much. It's true, I could drink one beer if I wanted and not go off the deep end. However, if one person saw me drinking, they might assume that if Pastor Larry drinks, it must be okay for them also. Do you realize what kind of message I would be sending? I would be giving others an opportunity to stumble, not to mention being used of the devil.

In addition to causing people to stumble, there are those who have had a problem with alcohol in the past that could be seriously affected by seeing a believer drink. If they were weak, it would be extremely difficult and possibly tempting to see another believer drinking. What's more, those who totally oppose drinking alcohol could stumble after seeing a believer drink. And finally, Christian parents who think it's okay to drink in front of their children must consider whether their lifestyle is the kind of example they want to set for their children.

This Scripture from Romans 14:21 is exactly why I don't drink alcohol. In fact, it doesn't matter whether I think it's a sin or not. The point is: Am I willing to do something that might offend a brother or sister?

People Became Offended at Jesus

Jesus made this statement in Matthew 15:10-12 that caused the religious leaders of His day to become offended at Him:

> *When He had called the multitude to Himself, He said to them, 'Hear and understand: Not what goes into the mouth defiles a man; but what comes out of the mouth, this defiles a man. Then His disciples came and said to Him, 'Do You know that the Pharisees were offended when they heard this saying?'*

Notice that as soon as Jesus spoke these words, His disciples asked Him if He was aware that the Pharisees were offended by what He spoke.

Perhaps you have thought that no one ever offended Jesus, or that He didn't have to tolerate the same kind of issues that we do. Or maybe you've had the impression that because Jesus was the Son of God, He possessed a special power to live without offense. But that's simply not true. Notice from Matthew 13:55-58 that the people who lived in His home town of Nazareth were offended by Him. It says:

> 'Is this not the carpenter's son? Is not His mother called Mary? And His brothers James, Joses, Simon, and Judas? And His sisters, are they not all with us? Where then did this Man get all these things?' So they were offended at Him.

In essence they were saying, "Who does He think He is? Isn't that the carpenter's kid who lived down the street? He thinks He's a hotshot because He has disciples following Him." The residents of Nazareth became offended at Jesus because of their familiarity with Him. At some point in your life, you may have become offended when a friend succeeded or received a position of prominence.

An Overly-Familiar Attitude

Some people can become offended at you for simply speaking the truth, but don't allow it to depress you or make you feel guilty. Remember, Jesus, who always spoke the truth, offended religious leaders. Jesus made this statement about the residents of Nazareth, who held an overly-familiar attitude toward Him: "A prophet is not without honor, except in his own country and in his own house" (Matthew 13:57). So, don't be surprised if your family, friends, or co-workers get offended at you in the same way. In fact, you can expect it.

Another example of an overly-familiar attitude can occur between a husband and wife. When a wife becomes overly-familiar with her husband, she may prefer going to the pastor or the elders of the church for prayer, instead of her husband. That can happen to any of us when we know the weaknesses and strengths of others. However, you can avoid becoming offended by familiarity by separating the person and all their weaknesses from the anointing that abides within them.

The natural, human things that everyone does, like leaving dirty socks on the floor, can cause those familiar with this behavior to question their spiritual abilities. A wife may ask herself, "How can I receive from this man when he doesn't even have enough sense to pick up his dirty socks?" However, when you separate the natural man from the anointing, you will be able to receive the Word of God from him.

Become aware of the possibility of offense occurring in your everyday life, then resist the temptation to be offended. Repeat this aloud: "Today, I forgive those who have wronged me. I let go of the offense that has clung to me for years. By faith, I release offense and let it go. By the power of God that works through me, I declare by faith that offense has to flee."

Chapter Nine

Godliness and Contentment:
A Link to Increase

The Apostle Paul said in Philippians 4:11, "Not that I speak in regard to need, for I have learned in whatever state I am to be content." We can determine that because Paul had to learn to be content, it is not a mind-set that automatically comes upon a Christian when he is born again.

Paul was not only referring to his surroundings when he spoke about contentment. Instead, Paul remained content no matter who he was in contact with — Christians or non-Christians, Jews or Greeks, those who loved or hated Jesus — it made no difference to him. He had learned to be content regardless of who or what was around him.

Can you say what Paul said? Can you remain content when someone says abrasive or hurtful words to you? Or do you come close to snapping at someone when an inappropriate word is spoken to you? Don't be discouraged by the way you answered these questions. If Paul could learn to be content, then so can you!

The Greek word for "learned" from this verse is *manthano* which means "learned and applied knowledge." In other words, the meaning of this word indicates that Paul had to learn to be content; it wasn't automatic. Some have the misconception that the Apostle Paul had a special anointing that protected him from things like offense, but Paul was human and dealt with the same emotions that you and I do. And consequently, just like you and me, he had to make the decision to be content.

The word "learned" also means "to learn by practice, to acquire the habit, to become accustomed to." This definition is especially important. Most of us have learned wrong behavior from our upbringing. We have practiced it all our lives, and it has now become a habit.

Some people's backgrounds have taught them to be offended, while others have been taught to be content. If you are one of those who have been taught to be offended, God's Word can help you acquire the habit of contentment. Any habit can be changed by renewing your mind with the Word of God. Romans 12:2 says, "Do not be conformed to this world, but be transformed by the renewing of your mind, that you may prove what is that good and acceptable and perfect will of God."

Godliness Comes from Obedience

Another misconception of many Christians is believing that godliness is imparted at the new birth. Instead, godliness comes from obedience to the Word of God. Paul said that you are to "...exercise yourself toward godliness" (1 Timothy 4:7). Who does the exercising? You do. Later in that same letter to Timothy, Paul charged us to pursue godliness (1 Timothy 6:11).

And remember, the Word says that the combination of godliness and contentment will produce great gain. Therefore, you can be confident that when you obey God and learn to be content, you can experience the supernatural in your life, just like the Apostle Paul did.

The Results of Ungodliness

Paul also admonished Timothy, his son in the Lord, about the consequences of not keeping with the doctrine of godliness. Notice what he said in 1 Timothy 6:3-6:

> *If anyone teaches otherwise and does not consent to wholesome words, even the words of our Lord Jesus Christ, and to the doctrine which accords with godliness, he is proud, knowing nothing, but is obsessed with disputes and arguments over words, from which come envy, strife, reviling, evil suspicions, useless wranglings of men of corrupt minds and destitute of the truth, who suppose that godliness is a means of gain. From such withdraw yourself.*

This may surprise you, but it says that if a person does not agree with wholesome words—only God's words are wholesome—and to the doctrine that supports godliness, then he is proud. A proud person exalts himself above others—considering himself superior to others.

In reality, a proud person compares himself with someone else and concludes that he measures up higher.

In addition to being proud, Paul makes a shocking statement regarding those who don't comply with wholesome words. He said "they *know nothing.*" If that's not enough of an insult, he said that a proud person is obsessed with disputes and arguments over words that come from envy, strife, reviling, evil suspicions, and useless wranglings of corrupt minds. He continues saying that this person is destitute of the truth, which means that they have absolutely no truth in them.

As a final warning, Paul clearly instructs believers to withdraw themselves from people who use godliness, or the presumption of godliness as a means of gain (v. 5). We are to literally back away from this kind of person and no longer associate with them.

Solomon, who was the wisest man in the world, validates this thought in Proverbs 13:20. He says, "He who walks with wise men will be wise, but the companion of fools will be destroyed." To put it very bluntly, if you associate with dummies, you'll start acting like a dummy. On the other hand, if you want to be wise, then you must begin associating with wise people.

The Absence of Contentment

Surely, you have been in a situation in which you lacked contentment — where things just didn't seem right. Maybe you were considering getting involved in a business deal, but something just didn't appear quite right. Or perhaps you were going to buy a car until you began to sense a disturbing feeling in your heart. Possibly you felt uneasy when a friend said that if you sign up with their company and get two people in your downline, you won't have to work again and you just might become a millionaire.

When something just doesn't sound right, it means that you have no peace or contentment. And when contentment is absent, there will be no gain. Surely you want to increase in your life, don't you?

I certainly want increase in every area of my life — in the knowledge of God, in the fellowship with my friends, in my relationship with my wife, in my relationship with my children, and of course, in my finances and my health. Basically, I want everything to be better tomorrow than it is today because that's what God wants. But if we expect to see increase, then we must realize it is linked with contentment.

Offense Denies You Peace

Living a life of contentment is your choice. So is living in offense. And, of course, offense will prevent you from being content. Not only will offense deny you contentment, but it can stop you from sleeping at night, from digesting food properly, and if that is not enough, it will cause great difficulty in your relationships.

Offense will also prevent you from working at peak performance in your job. You won't be able to think efficiently when working on your finances and paying your bills. Basically, when you lack contentment, you will not be all that God intends for you to be. Lastly, you will not be at peace in life when you are harboring offense in your heart.

Although we have all had wrong things done to us, what others do is of little importance. However, what *you* do is critical. There will always be someone who comes against you, or someone who will lie to you or lie about you. There will always be untrustworthy people who will try to steal from you. In fact, it doesn't matter how good a person you are, there will always be people who talk badly about you behind your back.

People criticized Jesus, lied about Him, and became offended with Him. And because they mistreated Jesus, they will mistreat you. Jesus warned about this ill-treatment in Matthew 10:24-25 saying,

> *A disciple is not above his teacher, nor a servant above his master. It is enough for a disciple that he be like his teacher, and a servant like his master. If they have called the master of the house Beelzebub, how much more will they call those of his household!*

Since Jesus was treated badly, what makes you think you can avoid these things? Certainly you don't consider yourself greater than the master, do you? Jesus said in John 16:33, "In the world you will have tribulation; but be of good cheer, I have overcome the world."

Although Jesus warned us that we would have trouble, His focus was on the fact that He overcame; therefore, we can overcome! The Apostle Paul was not only familiar with trouble, but he experienced victory as well. In 2 Corinthians 4:8-11, he described the attitude he held toward difficulty:

We are hard pressed on every side, yet not crushed; we are perplexed, but not in despair; persecuted, but not forsaken; struck down, but not destroyed — always carrying about in the body the dying of the Lord Jesus, that the life of Jesus also may be manifested in our body. For we who live are always delivered to death for Jesus' sake, that the life of Jesus also may be manifested in our mortal flesh.

Notice the uplifting way of thinking Paul maintained toward difficult times. He had every reason to be discontent; however, he chose to rejoice in the goodness of God.

Make the determination today to adopt Paul's attitude towards difficult times, as well as towards difficult people. Learn to be content regardless of the circumstances. And as you apply what you learn to godliness, you will begin to experience great gain.

Chapter Ten

Focus on Faith, Not the Problem

There are many ways in which people can become offended that are not so obvious, like being offended at places. I know someone who was so offended at the town in which they lived that they griped and complained about it constantly. Others have gotten offended at their car saying things like, "This car's nothing but a piece of junk." They spend much of their time complaining about their car.

Still others have harbored offense at someone who has been dead for decades. A woman in my church told me about being molested at the age of seven or eight by an uncle. Although he died thirty or forty years ago, this woman, who is now in her sixties or seventies, is still offended and thinks about her uncle every single day.

She is wasting her life sulking over the fact that he hurt her, but there is nothing she can do that can make him repay her. After all, what can he possibly do when he is no longer alive? There is nothing that can be done, there is no action that can be taken that will repair the damage that he did.

Justice and peace can only be received from one place, and that place is Jesus. But as long as she holds onto the offense, she will never find peace or contentment.

Faith is Single-Minded

If the devil can get you to focus on offense, he is able to hinder you, and he will prevent you from increasing in the things of God. Becoming engrossed in offense places you in bondage to the devil. When you are focused on a past hurt or offense, you are not living by faith because faith focuses on the promise and not the problem. Faith focuses on the answer from God instead of the circumstance.

Faith is single-minded — totally absorbed in one matter — God's promise. You either fix your eyes on what is good or what is bad, but you cannot give your attention to both simultaneously. In referring to a single-minded person, James 1:6-7 says,

> But let him ask in faith, with no doubting, for he who doubts is like a wave of the sea driven and tossed by the wind. For let not that man suppose that he will receive anything from the Lord.

On the other hand, an offended person is always negative, focusing on the problem instead of the answer. Unlike a person of faith, an offended person centers his attention on what is bad instead of what is good.

Have you ever noticed that an offended person asks negative questions like, "Why is this happening to me?" or "Doesn't God care for me?" Many times when people are consistently negative, they are covering something up. Their negativity is a facade for what is really happening on the inside—like protecting an offense.

Oddly enough, offended people frequently exalt themselves as a type of cover-up for their inner pain and suffering. Even though an offended person may talk like others are better then he is, in his heart he feels superior; otherwise, he wouldn't be offended. Philippians 2:3 deals with this attitude: "Let nothing be done through selfish ambition or conceit, but in lowliness of mind let each esteem others better than himself."

Offense will often manifest itself in jealousy, envy, or pride, and vice versa. This behavior becomes a cycle. When you get hurt, you immediately take offense. Then the offense creates a hurt, which becomes a deeper offense that leads to a greater hurt, and the cycle carries on. Life within this cycle never receives the fullness of what God has planned.

The Cycle of Offense

Many offended people never really feel like they are treated quite good enough. They may even feel that the reason good things don't happen to them is because society is out to get them. As a result, they are constantly moving from one unpleasant situation to another. For instance, they move from one relationship to another, always complaining about the last person who hurt and disappointed them. This kind of behavior only perpetuates the cycle of offense.

To break this cycle, you must reject the belief that everyone is out to get you. That is merely a lie from the devil and if you believe it, then you will play right into his trap. Refuse to expect something hurtful or wrong to be done to you. Don't allow the devil to keep you in that type of bondage. Living in offense can cost you your life, your family, your sanity, or your ministry.

In a previous chapter, we recognized the fact that offended people tend to change churches frequently. Of course, there are legitimate reasons for changing churches, like a desire to be with family or friends, a job transfer, or God calls you to a new place. These are among the various acceptable reasons for changing churches.

However, there are also unacceptable reasons for changing churches. For instance, some people church-hop because something a church does always offends them. They go to one church for awhile, but when something is done that they don't like, they change churches. These people can spend their entire lives floating from one church to another, always offended by the previous place. There is always something wrong with the last church that sends them seeking yet another place of worship. Moving from church to church is really no different than changing from one relationship to another—it's simply done on a larger scale.

A pattern of an offended person can also include switching from job to job. After being on the job for six or eight months, suddenly someone doesn't treat them right, and they become offended. A common mind-set of an offended person goes something like this: "How dare they treat me this way? I deserve better than this. I'll show them. I'll quit at rush hour when there is a long line at the cash register. They aren't going to push me around anymore."

Moving from one situation to another, whether it's friendship, a church, or employment, becomes a pattern in the life of an offended person. As you can plainly see, offense affects every aspect of life. Although it may be possible to hoodwink others about being offended, when it comes to dealing with the things of God, you won't get away with it.

The next time you wonder why things aren't going well, you might want to consider whether or not you are holding on to an offense that is preventing the blessing of God in your life. If you will be brutally honest with yourself, you will be able to recognize offense when it is hindering you. Then you can be set free!

We Are Commanded to Forgive

The first time I heard a message on offense, it offended me! I thought every example that the minister used in his message was being directed toward me. Once I became honest and realized that I held offense against certain people and things, I released it and was set free from bondage. What a tremendous feeling it is to be free!

Finally, I have grown to the point where I recognize things that would offend me and deal with them. Although the devil still brings opportunities to be offended my way, I resist them. I have learned to live in this place of contentment where God has something to work with! However, refusing to let go of offense is nothing more than disobedience.

Let me ask you a question. Who has offended you? Perhaps a malicious gossiper intentionally spread a rumor to hurt you. Regardless of the circumstances, in order to live in the freedom that God desires for you, you must forgive that person and let go of the offense. Many people think that they have a perfectly good reason for acting the way they do, but they are mistaken. We must all quit thinking that we are the exception to God's law, because we aren't. We have all been commanded to forgive—without exception.

Jesus did not suggest that you "try" to forgive. No, the Word of God doesn't say anything about trying to forgive. Instead, it simply makes the command to forgive. Forgiveness is not an option. You either obey God by forgiving or you disobey Him by refusing to forgive.

Revenge is a Manifestation of the Flesh

Don't forget, offense comes with a purpose—to destroy you and your anointing. John 10:10 says, "The thief comes to steal, kill, and destroy." Who does the thief want to steal from, kill, and destroy? *You!* And how can he do it? One way is by causing offense that leads to a grudge. Holding a grudge simply means that you hope for an opportunity to get revenge against the person that has offended you.

Some people, because of the smile on their face and the snap in their step, may not look or act offended. It can be a façade. Deep down inside, they are waiting for just the right moment to get revenge. Do you know what revenge is? Revenge is retribution—payback. It waits, biding its time, patiently waiting to get even—or better yet—get ahead! That's when the devil has a foothold in your life, and he can successfully carry out his mission to steal, kill, and destroy.

How does it make you feel when someone says something behind your back? Although a person of faith may not like what is said, they don't respond by their feelings. A Bible-believing Christian lives by faith, not by their feelings. Instead of surrendering to their emotions, they make the decision to live on a higher level than feelings, yielding instead to the fruit of the Spirit.

Living your life by what you feel will enable the devil to entrap you. When you are led by your feelings, you become ineffective for God. The Apostle Paul said this in regard to those who live by the flesh:

> *For those who live according to the flesh set their minds on the things of the flesh, but those who live according to the Spirit, the things of the Spirit.*
>
> *Romans 8:5*

The apostle further states, "Now the just shall live by faith; but if anyone draws back, my soul has no pleasure in him" (Hebrews 10:38). And finally Paul said in 2 Corinthians 5:7, "We walk by faith and not by sight."

When you make decisions based on offense, whether you realize it or not, you are being led by your feelings. If the devil can manipulate you into bondage with hurtful feelings, then he will put an offense around every corner just so he will gain control in your life. Immature Christians are led by their feelings, but mature Christians are led by their commitments to God and His Word. Will you let your feelings guide you or your commitment to God?

People-Pleaser or God-Pleaser

Living your life according to what people say about you will cause you to become a people-pleaser instead of a God-pleaser. Peter addressed this type of attitude when a religious leader strictly commanded him not to preach in Jesus' name. The essence of Peter's response was essentially, "Are we going to be pleasers of God or pleasers of men?" (Acts 5:29).

Peter was simply saying that each of us must make the decision whether we are going to please people or God. The choice belongs to each of us.

The only reason a people-pleaser will try to make others happy is to avoid offending them. Yet, when you make decisions based on whether others approve or not, you are being led by the flesh and not the Spirit of God.

The sooner you realize that you will never please everyone, the sooner you will stop trying and begin living a more content life. There will always be someone who will dislike your decisions and become offended. So why not make the decision once and for all to please God and forget what people think? Once you make that decision, then you will begin to increase—bearing fruit in everything you do.

Chapter Eleven

The Ball-and-Chain that Weighs You Down

The Apostle Paul made this statement relating to himself. "Brethren, I do not count myself to have apprehended, but one thing I do, forgetting those things which are behind and reaching forward to those things which are ahead" (Philippians 3:13).

It can become a great comfort to realize that the apostle, who wrote two-thirds of the New Testament, was not perfect. In fact, this verse implies that he didn't consider himself as having attained complete maturity in his lifetime. Then again, there was one thing he consistently practiced — forgetting the past and reaching forward to the future. This proves that we can never go forward with God as long as we are bogged down with the things of the past.

Paul continues affirming his resolve in verse 14, "I press toward the goal for the prize of the upward call of God in Christ Jesus." In other words, to run the race and receive the prize of victory, you must get free from the ball-and-chain that weighs you down! I am using the illustration of a ball and chain as a symbol for offense and unforgiveness in your life. This passage may explain why people can do everything right—like tithe, fast, pray, and volunteer at the church—yet with all they do, they still cannot seem to win the prize.

The Shackle of Unforgiveness and Offense

Let me give you an example of a person's situation that may help to clarify this idea. Have you ever wondered how someone can be anointed with oil, receive prayer from the elders of the church, work out three times a week, eat the most nutritious food, sleep an adequate number of hours each night and, yet, can still be plagued by illness? It seems as though they are doing everything right.

Although a person may appear to be doing everything just right, if they are harboring unforgiveness and offense in their heart, it can hinder the Word of God from working. Unforgiveness and offense act like a shackle that prevent a person from receiving to their full potential. Jesus said this about unforgiveness in Mark 11:22-26,

> *Jesus answered and said to them, 'Have faith in God. For assuredly I say to you, Whoever says to this mountain, "Be removed, and be cast into the sea," and does not doubt in his heart, but believes that those things he says will be done, he will have whatever he says. Therefore I say to you, whatever things you ask when you pray, believe that you receive them, and you will have them.'*

Notice the assurance Jesus provides us in verse 24 when He said, "Whatever things you ask when you pray, believe that you receive them, and you will have them."

While this promise in verse 24 is unconditional, verse 25 is not. It says, "And whenever you stand praying, if you have anything against anyone, forgive him, that your Father in heaven may also forgive you your trespasses."

Notice the open-ended terminology Jesus uses in verse 25: "forgive *anything* against *anyone*." Forgiving *anything* and *anyone* is all-inclusive. This is not limited to offense alone. Jesus is not only addressing offense but also unforgiveness, jealousy, envy, strife, and anything else you are holding against a person. If you have "anything against anyone" you must release it because if you do not forgive, then God will not forgive you.

That means when you are in need and you approach the throne of God for help, unforgiveness becomes a barrier between you and God that will prevent His help from reaching you. And that, I might add, is not a good place to be. No wonder people ask, and ask, and ask, yet never receive. It could be that there is unforgiveness, jealousy, envy, or strife in their heart.

Run with Endurance

You cannot run the race that is set before you when you are bogged down with the weight of sin. This may come as a shock to you, but unforgiveness and offense are sins. Hebrews 12:1 says,

> *Therefore we also, since we are surrounded by so great a cloud of witnesses, let us lay aside every weight, and the sin which so easily ensnares us. And let us run with endurance the race that has been set before us.*

At some point in time, someone is going to say or do something that hurts or offends you. Furthermore, as long as you are in this world, someone is going to try to cheat you or lie about you. Jesus said in John 16:33 "These things I have spoken to you, that in Me you may have peace. In the world you will have tribulation; but be of good cheer, I have overcome the world." We are subject to offense on a regular basis simply because we live in this world; the good news is that Jesus has overcome, so you don't have to let offense affect you.

Forgiving Doesn't Make You a Doormat

Some Christians think that living a life of forgiveness means that you have to lie down and let people walk all over you or steal from you. That's not at all what Jesus said. You can stand up for yourself without being offended.

For example, if someone commits a crime against you, ask the Lord's leading on whether or not to take them to court. God may tell you to extend grace and mercy because He is working in this person's heart. If that's the case, then don't press charges.

On the other hand, the Lord may instruct you to press charges. That's why it's vitally important to not only ask God, but also get clear direction from Him.

Regardless of whether the Lord instructs you to extend grace and mercy or prosecute, what's most important is that you do not become offended.

You might question whether you can release offense because it sounds so impossible, but the Bible says you can do all things through Christ who strengthens you (Philippians 4:13).

Satan's Strategy

On occasion, I have been asked how to recognize an offended Christian. That question is easily answered in Matthew 7:19-20. It says, "Every tree that does not bear good fruit is cut down and thrown into the fire. Therefore, by their fruits you will know them."

Simply put, you will be able to tell an offended Christian by what kind of fruit they produce in their life. When someone is trapped by past offense, they won't produce good fruit in their present life. Remember, offense and unforgiveness have to do with the past, but God works in the present.

Everything God does, He does now. Second Corinthians 6:2 says, "Now is the day of salvation," and Psalm 118:24 says, "This is the day the Lord has made." Once more, Hebrews 11:1 says, "Now faith is...." Faith is not tomorrow's faith or yesterday's faith. Faith is now! We must focus on today and abandon the hurts of yesterday. Let them stay in the past where they belong and refuse to bring them into the present.

The devil will try to keep you hurt over the past by whispering past hurts in your ear in an effort to bring them into your present again. For example, he will whisper, "Do you remember what so-and-so said about you last month? What about the way that other individual treated you a year ago? And neither of them have done anything to resolve it."

Satan's strategy is keeping you bound by reminding you about the hurts of the past, making you anxious in the present day, or causing you to worry about tomorrow. He speaks softly, saying, "What are you going to do? There is a family reunion in six months, and everyone in your household has been at each other's throats. Then there's a class reunion, and all those people who harassed you in school will be there." Satan will attempt to make you worry about something that will most likely never happen.

The Father of Lies

But remember, don't allow Satan to ensnare you with his devices. Second Corinthians 2:11 warns us, "Lest Satan should take advantage of us; for we are not ignorant of his devices."

Realize that one of Satan's devices is to bring up events from the past in order to fill today with unforgiveness and offense. If that doesn't work, he will bring anxiety and fear about the future to fill today with cares. All these are an effort to prevent God from having room to work in your life. John 8:44 has this to say about Satan,

You are of your father the devil, and the desires of your father you want to do. He was a murderer from the beginning, and does not stand in the truth, because there is no truth in him. When he

speaks a lie, he speaks from his own resources,
for he is a liar and the father of it.

Jesus warned us that Satan is a liar and the father of lies, so simply refuse to listen to him.

Chapter Twelve

Unrealistic or Unfulfilled Expectations

Many people don't like to admit it, but deep down in their hearts, they are offended with God. One reason people get upset with God is that they expected something that never happened, so they became hurt. I call this kind of offense unrealistic or unfulfilled expectations.

Naaman, a commander of the army of Syria, provides a perfect example of becoming offended because of unfulfilled expectations. Second Kings 5:1-14 records the miracle of Naaman, the leper, whose unfulfilled expectations nearly cost him the miracle that God had planned. Elisha, the prophet of God, told Naaman that if he would dip seven times in the Jordan River, then he would be healed of leprosy. But because Naaman was a very important man, he expected the prophet to make a fuss over him. Elisha could at least speak to Naaman face-to-face. But instead, Elisha sent instructions to Naaman through his servant, Gehazi. When things didn't happen the way Naaman expected, he became so offended that it almost cost him a miracle.

Naaman only consented to dip in the river because his servant reasoned with him, saying, "My father, if the prophet had told you to do something great, would you not have done it? How much more then, when he says to you, 'Wash, and be clean?'" As a result of Naaman's obedience, he was healed of leprosy.

Many people, like Naaman, have become hurt and offended because things haven't worked out the way they expected. They expected something to occur a particular way, and when it didn't happen as they imagined, they were left unfulfilled, disappointed, disillusioned, or brokenhearted.

Luke 4:18 records the public announcement Jesus made regarding the anointing that rested upon Him. He said, "The Spirit of the Lord is upon Me because He has anointed Me to preach the gospel to the poor. He has sent Me to heal the brokenhearted."

The Greek word for *heal* in this verse means, "to mend, to furnish completely, to fix completely." The fact that the Lord wants your heart completely mended and fixed is unmistakable. He does not want you struggling with offense or unforgiveness in your life. In reality, He doesn't want anything to hinder you.

Unrealistic Images

Quite often, people struggle with unrealistic expectations regarding their relationships, even marital relationships. Unrealistic relationships are easily fed by television, movies, or reading romance novels.

Hollywood paints a very unrealistic image of the way people actually live. You do realize that movies are idealistic stories, don't you?

Hollywood will even paint an unrealistic image of what your spouse is supposed to look like. Perhaps you expected your spouse to conduct his or her life the way a particular movie star behaves. When you get a preconceived idea of the way someone is supposed to behave toward you, your course is set for disappointment and ultimately, offense.

In other words, you can develop dreamlike fantasies about how people are supposed to behave by routinely watching the role of an imaginary person. You can even begin to plan for a mid-life crisis after watching a number of fictional characters experience it. But you don't have to experience a mid-life crisis unless you have been conditioned to believe that you do.

Positioned for Disappointment

When a man watches love and passion portrayed in movies, he begins to expect the same performance from his wife. For instance, when he comes home from a tough day at work, he expects his wife to be waiting in a black negligee, with her hair hanging attractively around her shoulders. Then she breathes out heavily, "I've been waiting for you." After all, this is how it goes in the movies, isn't it?

However, when this man comes home, instead of being greeted by Mrs. Voluptuous from the cover of a magazine, he finds his wife sitting on the couch next to an empty bag of potato chips with curlers in her hair. What men fail to realize is that it takes a professional artist hours, and hundreds of dollars, to airbrush all the flaws out of a model's face before appearing on the cover a magazine.

Have you ever seen a movie star or another famous person face-to-face? My son and I were going out on a 43 foot triple-engine boat in Sarasota, Florida, when a man jumped on the front of our boat and asked if he could go with us. Assuming he was the dock man untying the lines, we agreed.

When we were about a hundred yards from the dock, he looked up and said, "Oh boy, oh boy, show time." We looked up to find the media lining the dock, armed with movie cameras. My son and I didn't recognize the man in our boat who was completely gray except for the tips of his hair which had been dyed blond. He immediately took a baseball cap out of his hip pocket to cover his gray hair, leaving only the blond exposed. We soon discovered that the man on board our boat was a famous movie star. (I have to say, the man looked good even when he was pretending.)

It's easy to understand how many people expect their spouse to be Mr. or Mrs. Hollywood as a result of the unrealistic image that Hollywood paints, or why some parents expect their children to be Ricky and David Nelson. But real life is not like the Partridge Family.

Let go of any false images you may have had and begin living in the real world; otherwise, you will constantly experience hurt and offense that come from unrealistic and unfulfilled expectations. Although you can be healed of a broken heart caused by unfulfilled or unrealistic expectations, it is far better to avoid being hurt by misleading images altogether.

A Doer of the Word

It is possible that the reason you don't experience the manifestations of God's Word in your life is because you have held onto unrealistic expectations. Even though you may be fine in some aspects of life, you may not be at your full potential because you are angry with someone, possibly even with God. You may be offended at God because He didn't seem to perform like some preacher said He would.   •

Although Jesus has done everything needed to ensure your success when He shed His blood on the cross, you must still be a doer of the Word. James 1:22 says, "But be doers of the word, and not hearers only, deceiving yourselves."

God's will doesn't automatically come to pass in your life. No, *you* must implement the Word if you expect to see results. You are deceived if you think the Word only applies to someone else but not really to you. You cannot dismiss what God says with the excuse that it applies to someone else. Instead, you must take everything God says personally.

No one is an exception to the Word of God. The Word applies to everyone—including you and me. You must practice the Word in order to receive what He promises. Contrary to what some believe, being a Christian takes effort; it is not a free ride.

It may require a great deal of effort to release hurt and offense that you have harbored toward others, but it is the only way you will remove the obstacles that have prevented the blessing of God.

Offense and unforgiveness are the kiss of death to your relationships, your finances, and your ministry. Like a cancer, offense travels throughout your life, consuming all the healthy parts. When offense remains alive in your heart, you will be an unfulfilled, joyless person, regardless of the facade you put on at church.

Victory Over the Impossible

Although it may seem impossible to forgive those who have hurt you, it is not beyond the realm of the supernatural power of God. A woman in our church provides a perfect example of receiving victory over an impossible situation. This woman, who had won the Miss Shirley Temple look-alike contest in 1936, is one of the most wonderful, tenderhearted people I have ever met in my life. However, when she first came to the church, she had a lot of hatred and unforgiveness towards a man who had murdered her granddaughter, although he had never been apprehended. She also harbored wrong feelings toward God for allowing it to happen. It had caused her to be a bitter woman.

Although this woman's offense was justified, it was destroying her life nonetheless. Once she finally decided to release the offense she held towards the murderer, all she had to do was simply forgive him. By doing so, she cut off the life-source feeding the offense from the inside, rendering it powerless to destroy her. Now she can get up in the morning and have a wonderful day because the pain that came to destroy her has been removed. That doesn't mean that she liked what the murderer had done, or that she wanted to buddy around with him.

This woman's heart had been shattered, but Jesus healed her broken heart! Jesus died and shed His blood so that people, just like this woman, could be healed from the hurt and offense that comes to destroy them. If this woman could overcome the hurt caused by a murdered loved one, then you can triumph over whatever has hurt you.

The bottom line is that it doesn't matter what the offense is, once you make the decision to forgive and release it, Jesus will supernaturally make you whole.

This kind of miraculous power cannot be achieved with your own natural strength. The only way you can receive the ability to forgive is by the power of God working through you. The woman who forgave her granddaughter's murderer could not have done so by her own strength or will power. She had tried to forgive him before, but it required the supernatural power of God activated in her life. She stepped out in faith and said, "I'm turning this situation over to You, Father. I forgive the man even though he is guilty. I declare by faith that I no longer hate him or harbor unforgiveness toward him. I receive the anointing to heal my shattered, broken heart. Now I am free."

Ask in Faith

When she prayed that prayer, it was an act of faith on her part. She didn't necessarily feel any different, but

God took over and did what she could not do for herself. James 1:6-7 admonishes:

> *Let him ask in faith, with no doubting, for he who doubts is like a wave of the sea driven and tossed by the wind. For let not that man suppose that he will receive anything from the Lord.*

This woman was able to do the impossible because she asked in faith—refusing to rely on her feelings, but on the strength that Jesus Christ imparted. (See Philippians 4:13.)

Jesus said in Mark 9:23, "If you can believe, all things are possible to him who believes." This woman's impossibility became a possibility simply because she believed and acted on God's Word.

You can receive the same miraculous power that this woman experienced. Don't allow another day to go by harboring offense in your heart. As an act of your faith, pray a prayer similar to what this woman prayed, and you will begin your journey to freedom today!

Chapter Thirteen

Eradicate Fear, Unforgiveness, and Guilt

Have you ever been over-involved in an area that you thought was simply a passion, then after a while it seemed like it was almost an addiction, and eventually it became a way of life? At first you may simply begin by dabbling in an area, but it is Satan's goal to turn these innocent things into a deep stronghold in your life.

There are three key strongholds that Satan uses against every believer that must be eliminated from your life. Satan's mission is to derail you from the will of God, and he does it through bondage.

It is essential to understand that Satan—not God—is the one who oppresses people. Once again, John 10:10 says, "The thief does not come except to steal, and to kill, and to destroy. I have come that they may have life, and that they may have it more abundantly." Jesus only came to bring us abundant life and not destruction.

You can be bound physically, mentally, financially, or emotionally. Some people are bound by their relatives or the circumstances of life, while others are bound by religion. In any case, whenever people are bound, the devil is behind it. Paul and Silas were bound by shackles while in prison, but when the angel of the Lord showed up, they were set free. Jesus' mission is to release and set captives free!

The Lord said in John 8:31-32, "If you abide in my word, you are my disciples indeed. And you will know the truth, and the truth will set you free." We all want to be free from the things that hinder us, and if we expect to live an abundant, prosperous life, then we must be set free from the devil's bondage.

As I mentioned, there are three important strongholds that every believer must be released from. They are fear, unforgiveness, and guilt. These strongholds should never be a part of a Christian's life.

Number 1: Eliminate Fear

Fear is probably one of the most common strongholds that govern people. There are many different forms of fear. Some people fear the unknown, while others are fearful because of what they do know. Countless people are afraid of the future, whereas some are terrorized by the past. Others dread their current life.

Do you remember the Y2K panic? It was thought by many that in the year 2000 there would be a massive power failure. Some thought that all the banks were going to shut down, and the world system would collapse. However, my son-in-law is a senior scientist for the Department of Defense, and he laughed whenever anyone talked about Y2K.

Personally, I believed that on January 1, 2000, I would wake up in the morning and would see the sun come up in the east just like I always have. I was going to put on a pot of coffee because my coffeepot would work normally. I wasn't planning on having a disaster in my life.

Worldwide disaster should be irrelevant to you because you're a Christian and you believe the Word of God and God cares for you; therefore, there is nothing to fear!

Authority Over Fear

It is essential that believers understand that Jesus has given them authority over fear. This command is repeated throughout the Bible: "Fear not." Notice just a few Scriptures in which authority is given to those who are disciples of Jesus:

> 'Behold, I give you the authority to trample on serpents and scorpions, and over all the power of the enemy, and nothing shall by any means hurt you' (Luke 10:19).

> 'Assuredly, I say to you, whatever you bind on earth will be bound in heaven, and whatever you loose on earth will be loosed in heaven' (Matthew 18:18).

> Then He called His twelve disciples together and gave them power and authority over all demons, and to cure diseases (Luke 9:1).

If you consider yourself a servant of Jesus, then you will suffer the same insults He did. They accused Jesus of being of the devil, so they will accuse you of the same thing. Jesus said in Matthew 10:25, "It is enough for a disciple that he be like his teacher, and a servant like his master. If they have called the master of the house Beelzebub, how much more will they call those of his household?"

The most important part of this passage is found in the next verse. It reads, "Therefore do not fear them" (v. 26). You should underline that in your Bible. Jesus has given you authority over all the power of the enemy. So there is no reason to fear the devil, demons, or the people the devil uses.

Phobia

The Greek word "fear" in this verse is *phobio* which denotes terror, specifically the terror of men. It actually means "panic that grips a person causing him to run away, to be alarmed, to be filled with dread." If you have ever experienced that type of fear, you know just how disabling it is. Perhaps panic has gripped you in such a way that all you wanted to do was run away — run from your circumstances, from your home, from the problem, just run as far away as possible.

Dread

Dread is one of the most subtle, yet unbearable forms of fear. Can you imagine the dread that people felt long ago when their city was completely surrounded by enemy soldiers? No food or water could get in and no one could get out, while the army outside had plenty of food and water. All those inside the city suffered with the dread of certain defeat at any moment by the enemy.

First John 4:18 says that fear involves torment. Christians suffer needlessly with dread because they feel there is no way out of their problems. But they have believed a lie. Jesus will make a way where there seems to be no way. He said in John 14:6, "I am the way, the truth, and the life."

The Fear of Man

The fear of man is as destructive as the fear of God is constructive. Proverbs 29:25 says, "The fear of man brings a snare, but whoever trusts in the Lord shall be safe." People without a covenant with God live in fear and will always try to make you as fearful as they are. But the fear of man will always result in a snare. The fear of man will lure you into a trap that the devil has set for you. As long as you live your life fearful of man, you will be continually caught in snares.

However, according to this verse the only thing you must do to be safe is trust in the Lord. The word "trust" in this verse means to have faith. It would be just as appropriate to say that to remain safe you must have faith in God. That means you must believe and act on what God says and the results will be safety.

The Fearful Are the Faithless

In Mark 11:22 Jesus said, "Have faith in God." We understand that in the Hebrew language, faith and fear are opposites. Like opposing sides of a magnet, you cannot center your attention on faith and fear at the same time. You may assume you're acting in faith, but if fear is present you cannot be in faith. And without faith—the catalyst required to activate the Word of God—you will not benefit. Faith must be present and active if you desire to prosper.

Notice the writer of Hebrews stresses the possibilities to those who have had the gospel preached to them.

> *For indeed the gospel was preached to us as well as to them; but the word which they heard did not profit them, not being mixed with faith in those who heard it.*
>
> *Hebrews 4:2*

There is an obvious advantage to hearing the gospel preached, yet if you don't add your faith to it, you will not prosper from what you heard. Therefore, it can be concluded that the root of lack and deficiency is unbelief. The Word is only profitable to those who believe.

If the devil can keep you fearful, he will succeed in keeping you faithless because it is impossible to operate in both fear and faith simultaneously. As long as you are in unbelief, the Word of God will not work for you.

This principle applies in every area of life. For example, if you don't have faith for Christ's ability to save you, you will not be born again. Or you could say Christ's death won't profit you. Ephesians 2:8 says, "For by grace you have been saved through faith." Faith is required to activate the Word of God in your life for salvation. Without the catalyst called faith, new life will not be imparted.

As long as you remain fearful, you will not operate in the things of God. First John 4:18 says, "There is no fear in love, but perfect love casts out fear, because fear involves torment. But he who fears has not been made perfect in love." The only way to conquer fear is to immerse yourself in God's love. Then fear will flee and faith can begin to develop.

Don't Miss the Good Things

Have you ever missed something good because you wouldn't change? I have. In fact, there are two things that I have missed. The first is iced tea, and the second is peanut butter. But once, when I lost my voice, my wife gave me tea with lemon and honey. When I tasted it for the first time I realized that it tastes good. I guess I'll try peanut butter next!

My point is that many people miss good things simply because they will not change. Some people will simply stick to a belief or a denomination strictly because of tradition, pride, or stubbornness — "My daddy, like his daddy, was a Presbyterian and all my family members are Presbyterians no matter what the Bible says!" But something is wrong when you will not receive the things of God because of tradition or what your friends or family members might say.

Instead of being withheld because of tradition, pride, or stubbornness, you must reach a point in your life when you look to the Word of God and stop filtering what is said about the Bible through denominational eyes. Lay aside tradition and look to the Word of God alone. Ask yourself the question "Do I believe something just because my church or family believes it, or do I believe it because God said it?"

Have you ever wondered if it's possible that God has said exactly what He meant? Some people treat God's Word like a newscaster who explains what the politician really meant after he makes a great speech. Is it possible that the politician said what he meant and we don't need a newscaster to explain it?

Change Requires Commitment

Most people fear change because change requires a commitment. For believers who desire to get closer to the Lord, the decision to change also involves acting on your commitment.

But fear will always say, "You can't change. You have always been this way, and you always will be. Why bother trying?" Perhaps fear has told you that if you sell out to God, then you will lose all your friends. Or fear might accuse you of becoming "too heavenly-minded for any earthly good." In fact, if you get too close to God, your church might give you the left foot of fellowship.

This is what fear does. It will keep you away from the things of God, utilizing all your waking hours on worry. Fear will fill your heart with anxiety and cause you to be ineffective for God because you will be too busy being fearful.

Second Timothy 1:7 says, "For God has not given us a spirit of fear, but of power and of love and of a sound mind." Fear should never be a part of a believer's life because the Bible says that God has not given you a spirit of fear. That means a spirit of fear comes from the devil.

You don't have to live in fear, but when it has become a stronghold in your life, it is like a boulder that cannot be gently nudged out of the ground. Instead, it takes a crowbar, called faith in the Word of God, to give it a big push to snap it out of the ground. The Word of God can do that for you.

We are living in a sliver of time just before the return of Jesus, and there isn't time to nurture you for ten, fifteen, or twenty years to remove fear. This is the age when God is doing a fast work. If you don't think it's time for Jesus to return, then you haven't been watching the news because prophecy is being fulfilled everyday. God has a work for you to do, so if you're being controlled by fear, break free from it today.

Number 2: Eradicate Unforgiveness

When someone deeply hurts you, quite often it leaves you with the feeling that they owe you something. Most of the time, the people who hurt you don't realize what they have done. Do you really think others are planning their life around hurting you? Actually, very seldom does someone intentionally set out to hurt another person, although it can happen. Typically they hurt you when they are insensitive, rude, or angry at someone else. Meanwhile, you are so mad that you cannot even watch a good television show without stewing over the situation.

While you're miserable, they are eating at Shoney's, having a good time, and not even thinking about you. They are enjoying a piece of pumpkin pie with whipped crème on it while you're at home taking Tums, trying to keep the pain in your stomach under control.

While counseling a married couple, the wife accused her husband saying, "You owe me." Although he had hurt her for fifteen years, it was not within his power to give those years back to her. When somebody owes you a debt that they cannot pay, the only thing you can do is forgive the debt because it's not within human power to change the past.

Another woman hated her deceased father who had molested her. She refused to forgive him because she felt like he owed her because he had stolen her innocence. I couldn't help but think, *How much does he owe you? What are you going to do, dig up his grave and pawn the gold ring off his finger? He can't pay you back; he is gone.*

Forgiveness means to absolve from payment or to cancel a debt. If you have been seriously hurt, you might as well forgive and cancel the debt because there is nothing you can do to change the past. How long do you plan to live with the pain in your heart? Although you cannot change the past, you can change your response to it.

Forget the Past

When somebody uses the excuse that they cannot help what they think, it's not true. Remember the Apostle Paul said, "One thing I do, forgetting those things which are behind and reaching forward to those things which are ahead." Everyone has the ability to control their thoughts. If your thoughts couldn't be controlled, then Philippians 4:8 wouldn't instruct you what to think about. It says,

> *Finally, brethren, whatever things are true, whatever things are noble, whatever things are just, whatever things are pure, whatever things are lovely, whatever things are of good report, if there is any virtue and if there is anything praiseworthy — meditate on these things.*

You have the ability to choose what you will think about. You can think about the offense or you can choose, like the Apostle Paul, to forget what lies behind and press for what lies ahead.

When Jesus hung on the cross, He made a most amazing statement regarding forgiveness. In Luke 23:34 He said, "'Father, forgive them, for they do not know what they do.'" If Jesus didn't hold anything against the people who were responsible for His death, certainly you can release those who have offended you. Make the decision to release hurt today. Make today the day you get set free!

Number 3: Eliminate Guilt

Fear focuses on the future, unforgiveness focuses on the present, and guilt focuses on the past. Fear and unforgiveness have the ability to develop guilt. Satan is the king of guilt. He will try to destroy you by harassing you with the past.

A person that is full of guilt doesn't believe what God has done for him. Second Corinthians 5:21 says,

"For He made Him who knew no sin to be sin for us, that we might become the righteousness of God in Him." If you truly believed what God has done, then you would know that you are in right standing with God and that nothing can separate you from His love (Romans 8:38-39).

Notice the following Scriptures that tell you who you are and what you can do in Christ:

"I can do all things through Christ who strengthens me" (Philippians 4:13).

"But we have the mind of Christ" (1 Corinthians 2:16).

"You are of God, little children, and have overcome them, because He who is in you is greater than he who is in the world" (1 John 4:4).

And you, being dead in your trespasses and the uncircumcision of your flesh, He has made alive together with Him, having forgiven you all trespasses, having wiped out the handwriting of requirements that was against us, which was contrary to us. And He has taken it out of the way, having nailed it to the cross.
Colossians 2:13-14

Feelings of guilt come from your past, and they are designed to keep you from moving forward. The moment you start believing what the Word says about you, guilt will leave.

Far too many Christians suffer from fear, unforgiveness, and guilt. But God wants this year to be the year of restoration and recovery for you. And what makes restoration and recovery possible? Eradicating fear, unforgiveness, and guilt.

Chapter Fourteen

Offense in the Ministry

O ur church produces a large number of people who desire to go into the ministry. In fact, we have many licensed ministers in our church. But I have observed that some people get out of the ministry almost as quickly as they got in.

Regretfully, it's not uncommon for a minister to get offended at either people in the church or God because of very unrealistic expectations regarding the ministry. Far too often, people expect certain things to happen because they are in ministry and when they don't happen, they become offended at God.

For instance, some people imagine that things like offense, unforgiveness, worry, stress, and even financial problems will just go away after they become a licensed minister or once they have a church or ministry. But it's not that way at all. If you have a problem overcoming unforgiveness, offense, or financial bondage before you go into the ministry, then you might not survive the ministry.

It's not being in the ministry that liberates you from problems. Instead, it's the power of the Word of God working in you, and your willingness to allow the Holy Spirit to work through you. Ephesians 3:20 says that God is able to do exceedingly abundantly above all that we ask or think, but it's "according to the power that works in us." It has nothing to do with where you are employed.

The ministry is not the cure-all for the problems in your life. You will carry all your problems into any job you have unless you get rid of them. Changing occupations is not going to help. Your problems don't change when your occupation does. You must decide that you are going to get rid of offense before you go into ministry.

An Unrealistic Viewpoint

If you are planning to go into ministry, I highly recommend that you go to a Bible training school because most people who go into the ministry don't have a clue what it's all about. Otherwise, you risk becoming offended as a result of having unrealistic expectations.

I met someone who wanted to be a pastor because he envisioned only working two hours on Sunday morning and one hour mid-week. Perhaps, he thought there will be an occasional ministerial gathering over coffee with other brothers in the faith. I suppose the rest of the time he thought he could sit around the donut shop!

Some people really have that kind of impractical attitude. In fact, I asked one man why he was a pastor and he answered, "To be quite honest, I'm too lazy to work and too nervous to steal. The only thing left was to pastor."

That is the worst reason for being in ministry that I have ever heard! You are either called into ministry or you're not. An individual that is in the ministry for any other reason is sure to end in disaster.

There is no way to run a ministry while you are offended. You can try, but you will either live a miserable existence or you will fail. Ministers must have a pure heart before God so the people they minister to can trust them.

It doesn't take long after talking to a minister to tell if he is walking by faith or if he is walking in offense. Sometimes, moments after meeting them, they're talking about a deacon who did something wrong in their church or a group of people who are trying to run him out. A minister who speaks like this is holding offense against the people he is supposed to serve. This kind of attitude will never produce a prosperous ministry.

Quit Worrying About People

If I spent my time worrying about what my church members thought about me, I wouldn't get much accomplished for the Kingdom of God. The truth is, I don't care what they think. Even though I love them all, I am not going to cry about what someone may or may not think about me. If I do that, I will certainly become offended.

However, I have actually been around preachers who were seriously concerned about who did or did not shake their hand or what the deacon did or said. In fact, if a person like this sees two people on the pulpit committee talking in the back of the church, he immediately thinks he is about to lose his job, and he starts whining to deacons.

Most ministers endeavor to keep their hearts pure before God, but offense can sneak up on you, and slowly begin to grow into a serious problem. Suddenly you realize that you have been avoiding someone at the grocery store, or staying away from certain places, or refraining from particular activities, dreading a possible confrontation with the individual you hold adverse feelings toward.

Once offense or hurt has successfully penetrated your heart, it will fester and will become rancid. That's when you start having thoughts that begin to influence your daily plans. Suddenly you realize what has happened, and you can't imagine how you allowed yourself to get into that position.

When I first heard a message on offense, I realized that I had been holding onto some things all of my life. Once I was taught to release the offenses before God and I obeyed, God gained greater access into my life, enabling Him to move in and through me more powerfully.

I remember lying in bed several years ago, thinking about a man who had hurt my family. I was actually thinking about how I could destroy him.

I know what you're thinking: *A minister wouldn't think something like that.* It doesn't matter who you are—minister or lay person—no one is exempt from temptation. Anyone can have those thoughts unless they recognize the truth and ask God for forgiveness. Finally, several years later, I forgave this man and released the ill feelings that I was harboring against him. Now I am offense-free. It's so liberating to know that I can go anywhere or do anything, and it doesn't matter who I might run into.

Church Splits

Statistically, it has been said that the average church has a split within two years. Therefore, when we started our church, we made the decision from the beginning that we simply would not allow offense in it. Being the leader in the ministry, that decision had to come from me. As a result, I made a personal promise that no one would be able to offend me, no matter how hard they tried. If you are the leader of a ministry, you are responsible for making this same decision.

I refuse to be upset because the wrong flagpoles were ordered or the wrong banner is hung. I'm going to be happy no matter what the flagpole or banner looks like. I'm going on with God. And we can all go together if we refuse to become offended.

You can make an agreement with those involved in your ministry, like I did, that when someone does something goofy, you will be quick to forgive. If you will make the decision to get along and to love one another, you will be fine.

Talk Face-to-Face

At our church, we have a lot of sessions where we talk with one another. I have talked face-to-face with probably ninety percent of the people in my church at some point in time. We endeavor to keep the lines of communication open.

However, I am not indicating that you are supposed to be a garbage pail for others to dump their trash in. As a minister, when you open your life up to others, someone might try to use you to dump their problems on. But don't become a garbage collector for other people's offenses.

Whenever I realize that someone is using me to unload their garbage, I graciously turn the conversation in another direction. In the first place, I don't want someone else's garbage poured out on me. And secondly, it won't help the person who's unloading unless they make the decision to act on the Word.

Enjoy the Liberty of a Clean Heart

If you are in the ministry and you have offense toward anyone, you can be set free from bondage if you will act on the knowledge of the Word of God. Jesus said in John 8:31-32, "If you abide in My word, you are My disciples indeed. And you shall know the truth, and the truth shall make you free."

Pray and release unforgiveness today. You will not only begin to enjoy the liberty that a clean heart produces, but God will begin to move more powerfully through you.

Chapter Fifteen

You Can Have Great Peace

Psalm 119:165 says, "Great peace have those who love your law: and nothing causes them to stumble." The word *stumble* in this verse can also be translated "offend." Wouldn't it be great to live your life so that nothing offended you, just to go through one day of your life and not get mad, frazzled, or feel a flash of anger?

For example, for many divorced people it would be a huge victory to see their "ex" in the grocery store unexpectedly, and instead of reacting like a "psycho," actually feeling peace. Even though they might still remember the events they went through, their emotions don't have to control them.

You can live in great peace so that when you are face-to-face with someone who has hurt you, you remain calm and peaceful instead of going ballistic. And that will feel much better than anger or resentment. This kind of rest and joy is available to you regardless of what has happened in the past.

Some people might still be thinking, *But you don't know what happened to me. Things were good for thirty years, and then this person flipped out on me.* Remember, you cannot change what has happened in the past, but you can begin to realize how offense affects you spiritually, emotionally, and physically.

The Word says that you can have great peace, but this kind of peace doesn't come automatically. It only comes to those who love the law of God. And when you love the law of God, nothing—not a few things—it says *nothing* shall offend you.

If you have ever wondered whether or not you truly love the law of God, asking yourself this one question may forever resolve that uncertainty. Ask yourself, "Do I have great peace, or do I have a burr under my saddle about something?"

Examine Yourself

For instance, if someone said something really rude to you, how would you deal with it? First, you should examine yourself to see if what was said is true (1 Corinthians 13:5). Or if you really want to know, ask your spouse. They will tell you the truth! If what was said to you is true, then go to God in repentance and deal with it. And you should be grateful in your heart to the person who had the courage to tell you, whether they meant it for your good or not.

On the other hand, if you examine yourself and realize that what someone said to you was not true, you still have to deal with it. But instead of dealing with it by repenting before God, you will deal with it by forgiving the person for making false accusations. Otherwise, once the devil finds out what it takes to push your buttons, he can detour you from the will of God indefinitely. He will send offensive people across your path and keep you riled up so you won't influence anyone for God.

I have had people say things about me that were a total fabrication—simply a lie. It made me think to myself, *I cannot believe they said that.* That's when the temptation to get back at them arises. But if I had acted on the temptation, I would have taken hold of Satan's bait. Notice what the Apostle Paul said in 1 Corinthians 10:13 about temptation:

> *No temptation has overtaken you except such as is common to man; but God is faithful, who will not allow you to be tempted beyond what you are able, but with the temptation will also make the way of escape, that you may be able to bear it.*

While none of us are exempt from temptation, God has made a way for each of us to escape the temptation. The important thing is that we must choose to take that way of escape instead of our own way. Sometimes we have to make that choice in split-second timing.

Replace Negative Feelings with Peace

Although it is a wonderful feeling to see a person who has historically triggered negative emotions without having any unpleasant feelings toward them, it's even better to replace the negative feelings with great peace! Destructive emotions no longer have to dominate you.

When you release offense, it can be replaced with great peace. Notice that the Word doesn't describe it as "ordinary peace;" instead it characterizes it as "great peace." (Although for some, ordinary peace would be a welcomed option!)

The peace that the psalmist is referring to is supernatural peace. Jesus declared in John 14:27 that the world could not gain access to this kind of peace. He said,

> *Peace I leave with you, My peace I give to you; not as the world gives do I give to you. Let not your heart be troubled, neither let it be afraid.*

This verse is referring to super-strength peace. For example, a store may sell regular strength aspirin to manage an ordinary headache. They also sell an extra strength pain reliever to alleviate a more serious headache. In addition, they sell a magnum strength painkiller for migraine headaches.

Princely Peace

The literal translation of Psalm 119:165 indicates that this kind of great peace is a noble and princely peace. What kind of peace do you suppose a prince would have? When your birthright is of royal ancestry, you have extraordinary peace because you know that everything is under control. Peter pronounces that heritage on us:

> *But you are a chosen generation, a royal priesthood, a holy nation, His own special people, that*

*you may proclaim the praises of Him who called
you out of darkness into His marvelous light.*

1 Peter 2:9

As a born-again believer, you can have princely peace because your lineage is a royal priesthood. God has chosen you and has adopted you into His family. You now have God's blood flowing in your veins. What can hurt or upset you when you know God is on your side? Romans 8:31 says, "What then shall we say to these things? If God is for us, who can be against us?"

Nothing Shall Hurt You

Although the Word says that loving the law of God will give you great peace, the devil can use anything as a stumbling block against you. And, when you don't exercise your God-given authority over the devices of the enemy, offense can cause you to lose your balance. In Luke 10:19, Jesus entrusts you with authority:

*Behold, I give you the authority to trample on
serpents and scorpions, and over all the power of
the enemy, and nothing shall by any means hurt
you.*

Jesus has given believers authority over *all* the power of the enemy, and *nothing* by any means can harm you. Cruel words and insults cannot harm you. Wicked deeds have no damaging power over you. Insensitive people are harmless against you. Nothing offensive can harm you! Because of this authority, you are in control and that brings peace!

Remember, that doesn't mean you allow people to walk on you. There is a vast difference between being a doormat and *choosing* to forgive. Just because you refuse to take offense, doesn't mean you're a noodle! Actually, you will be demonstrating great strength.

Choose to live in your God-given authority, and the Bible promises that nothing by any means shall hurt you!

Chapter Sixteen

Six Steps to Living Offense-free

I'm sure you have heard a preacher spend an hour telling you how badly you needed to do something, and all the while you were thinking, *Okay, but how do I do it?* It's one thing to know what you are supposed to do, but it's entirely different knowing how to achieve it.

One time when I told a gentleman that he needed to let go of offense, he said, "I know I am supposed to let it go, but how do I? What's the process involved?" As a result of that conversation I would like to give you a six-step process to living offense-free.

Step 1: Develop hope for your deliverance

Hebrews 11:1 says, "Now faith is the substance of things hoped for, the evidence of things not seen." Faith is the firm foundation upon which your hope is built. You could say that faith is the title deed for the things you hope to see happen in your life.

Notice that hope alone does not contain the power to make impossible situations possible. It takes faith in God's Word to accomplish the impossible. In order to see your expectation realized, you must find out what God says about the situation and begin to apply your faith in that direction.

"Bible hope" can be defined as the expectation of the good things that God has promised you. Hope understands that you don't physically have what you desire, but when hope is coupled with faith, a powerful force exists that is stronger than any adverse situation.

For example, I spoke with a woman who said that before she went to church, she had no hope for her marriage. Although going to church did not solve the problem, hearing the Word of God created the ability to build the power of hope when things appeared hopeless. Something she heard gave her the hope that a place of peace was available. Hearing the Word of God creates hopeful expectation.

I have spoken to others who were facing bankruptcy, and it looked like there was no way out. That is a desperate place to be, but when the light of the Word of God shines in your darkness, you begin to realize that there is a way out in Jesus. John 14:6 assures us that Jesus is the way!

Your hope will grow when you confess God's Word. Speak the following verses out loud:

"I can do all things through Christ who strengthens me" (Philippians 4:13).

"All things are possible to him that believes" (Mark 9:23).

So the Lord said, 'If you have faith as a mustard seed, you can say to this mulberry tree, "Be pulled up by the roots and be planted in the sea," and it would obey you' (Luke 17:6).

And I will give you the keys of the kingdom of heaven, and whatever you bind on earth will be bound in heaven, and whatever you loose on earth will be loosed in heaven (Matthew 16:19).

Offended people are in desperate need of the power of Bible hope. Without God's supernatural intervention, some people may never live offense free. That is why it is essential to read and confess God's Word and develop hope for your deliverance.

Step 2: Personalize the Word of God

You must believe that the Word of God is literally God speaking to you. When you personalize what God says, you will receive revelation knowledge of who you are in Christ and what God has done for you. Then the supernatural peace of God will be revealed to you.

Many years ago, I had a lot of sleepless nights because I was facing financial ruin. It was so bad that I started bleeding internally. Nobody knew of my financial condition or my physical condition because I acted like everything was fine.

One evening, I asked Loretta, "What is the worst thing that could happen to us?" After a short discussion, we decided that the worst thing that could happen would be that we would lose everything, but we could handle that because God's Word is true. We could always start over. Suddenly I wondered why I was worrying at all.

When I began reading the Word of God, I discovered that God had said good things about me, but I hadn't been listening to Him. Instead, I was listening to the devil saying, "You're going bankrupt!" Just as soon as I started listening to God say He has given me abundance, everything turned around.

Whomever you choose to listen to, will affect what happens to you. Begin listening to what God's Word says and take it personally.

Step 3: Use common sense

Whenever possible, remove yourself from the person who offends you. Second Thessalonians 3:6 says,

> But we command you, brethren, in the name of our Lord Jesus Christ, that you withdraw from every brother who walks disorderly and not according to the tradition which he received from us.

Withdrawing from someone doesn't necessarily mean that you are judging, condemning, holding offense, or getting revenge. Proverbs 13:20 says, "He who walks with wise men will be wise, but the companion of fools will be destroyed." This verse indicates that who you associate with will affect you.

For example, it wouldn't be wise to associate with someone who is a wonderful Christian but is irritating to you. Befriending him wouldn't prove that he doesn't irritate you. That's asking for trouble! In this situation, it would be wise to remove yourself from an irritating person, if possible. Use common sense!

Step 4: Make a decision to forgive

The mind is where all battles are fought. Thus, before you can live offense-free, you have to make the decision to forgive. Luke 6:37 says, "Judge not, and you shall not be judged. Condemn not, and you shall not be condemned. Forgive, and you will be forgiven."

Notice, the very next verse begins by saying, "Give...." This is referring to giving the things in the previous verse—if you give judgment, you will receive judgment as well. If you condemn others, you will be condemned in return. However the good news is, if you forgive others, then you will also be forgiven and you won't be judged. In addition, in the same measure you give it, you are going to receive.

This process is commonly called the law of reciprocity—whatever you give is what you will receive. So, if you have been wondering why you've been so offended by others, then you might examine how much offense you have been giving out lately.

Sometimes offense comes not because you were hurt but because your children were. Taking on someone else's offense can be harder to let go of than your own.

Have you ever heard anyone say, "If you do something to me I can live with it. But if you do something to my wife or children, you'd better get on the next train out of town because I'm coming after you."

Does making the decision to forgive mean that you have forgiven? No, it simply means that you've taken the first step. Decisions are made in your mind. At first, you may still feel disgusted when you see the person, but you have to mentally decide that you are going to forgive and let go of the offense.

Perhaps the person genuinely doesn't deserve to be forgiven. Or maybe he hasn't asked for forgiveness. However, asking for forgiveness is not the condition set out in the Word. There are times when people cannot ask for forgiveness because they are no longer alive. Actually, it has nothing to do with someone asking for forgiveness, but it has everything to do with *you* getting free from the torment that accompanies offense.

If you are still arguing that you cannot, then you have already lost the battle. When you say you cannot forgive, you have actually made the decision that you won't forgive. *You* decide whether or not you are going to do something.

You cannot continue to cry over spilled milk or put toothpaste back in a tube. But you can forgive and begin living stress-free, offense-free, happy in the morning, smiling in the afternoon, and still smiling in the evening. But it takes a decision to forgive. No if's, and's, or but's about it. No excuses. No more "But, but, but...." You either make the decision to forgive or you don't.

Step 5: State your case

Once you have made the decision to forgive, then you must state your case with your words. Even if you have to say it a thousand times before you believe it, you must begin to speak forgiveness with your mouth. Whenever your mind thinks something contrary to the Word of God, simply refuse to say what you're thinking—keep saying what the Word says.

Let me give you an example of how this works. When you decide to buy a car you may think, "I cannot afford to buy a car. How am I going to pay for it?" But when the salesman asks, "Are you going to buy this car?" although you're still thinking you shouldn't, you answer, "Yes!"

Your mind is reasoning completely opposite from what your mouth has said. Although you are thinking about all the reasons why you shouldn't, you keep your thoughts inside and answer the salesman with a resounding, "Yes!" And because you said "yes" even though your mind said "no," your actions followed your words. You signed the papers and left with a new car. You now have a car, in spite of what you were thinking, because your words overrode your thoughts.

There is power in your words. Proverbs 18:21 says, "Death and life are in the power of the tongue, and those who love it will eat its fruit." When you say that you forgive out loud—although you may be thinking something else—you are getting your words in line with God. His supernatural power will cause it to come to pass. Keep doing it because eventually forgiveness will take root deep down inside your heart.

Matthew 5:44 tells us "Love your enemies, bless those who curse you, do good to those who hate you, and pray for those who spitefully use you and persecute you." Once, when a woman told me about her problems, she said, "I pray for my enemies." So I said, "Let's pray for them right now." I grabbed her hands, and she prayed "Dear Father, in the name of Jesus, bring pestilence and disaster upon them. Destroy them, Father. Poison their water."

I thought, *Wait a minute, when the Bible says pray for your enemies that's not what it's talking about.* She was serious! Her idea of praying for her enemies was a whole lot different than what the Bible says. We are to pray good things for them.

State your case with your words even if you have to say it two thousand times, but don't quit.

Step 6: Continue to believe

Finally, you must continue to believe and confess that God will heal your hurt. Continue to confess that you will forgive the one who offended you in spite of how you feel.

If you ever quit, you haven't obeyed God. Have you ever heard someone say, "I tried that but it didn't work." If things didn't change right away, they just quit. They might have hung in for a while, but we're talking about forever. Besides, forgiveness is not something you try. The Word doesn't say try to forgive and you'll be forgiven. No, it simply commands us to forgive.

What do you do when Satan tells you, "You can't forgive. It's impossible"? Rejoice! Because if the devil says you cannot do it, then you know you can because he's a liar (John 8:44). And Philippians 4:13 says, "You can do all things through Christ." All things includes forgiving. You can let go of offense. You can walk free from hurt into God's peace. You can do all things!

Although complete restoration with a person is possible, forgiveness is not based on whether or not restoration ever takes place. And if you are restored to the person, don't needle them for the rest of their life over what they did. Letting go of the offense means you must let it go forever.

Some people wrongly believe that forgiveness means that you condone the person's actions or that you accept what they did, but that is not true. God will punish the offender for the deeds done, but that punishment does not come from you. We know from Deuteronomy chapter 28 that obedience receives a reward and that disobedience receives punishment. Take for example Ananias and Sapphira, who received the consequences for their conduct.

Does that mean God is bad? Absolutely not! God is a good and just God. When the government imprisons people for breaking the law, does it mean that the government is bad? No, the government is enforcing justice when they incarcerate unlawful people in order to protect innocent people from harm.

Anyone can avoid punishment through simple obedience. However, if you have been disobedient, after you ask God's forgiveness, you must change. The Word says that the blood of Jesus cleanses you from all unrighteousness. That means that there is no unrighteousness whatsoever in you. As far as God is concerned, you are squeaky clean, just as though you had never sinned.

A quick review:

Six Steps to Living Offense Free

Step 1: Develop hope for your deliverance

Step 2: Personalize the Word of God

Step 3: Use common sense

Step 4: Make a decision to forgive

Step 5: State your case

Step 6: Continue to believe

Chapter Seventeen

The Answer to Offense

According to Galatians 5:6, in order for faith to work, we must act in love. It says, "For in Christ Jesus neither circumcision nor uncircumcision avails anything, but faith working through love." If you are offended at someone and are unwilling to forgive them, then the love of God isn't active in your life.

Who exactly are we supposed to love? Are we allowed to exclude the people who offend us? Jesus answered those questions in Matthew 5:44. He said, "But I say to you, love your enemies, bless those who curse you, do good to those who hate you, and pray for those who spitefully use you and persecute you." God commands us to love even the unlovely.

This passage instructs you to do something that in your own effort is impossible: love your enemies and pray for those who use and persecute you. To love like that takes a supernatural love—the God-kind of love. It will also require you to walk by faith and not by your feelings.

The love of God includes everyone, whether you consider them lovely or unlovely. You either act in love or you don't. There is no gray area. First John 4:20-21 says,

> *If someone says, 'I love God,' and hates his brother, he is a liar; for he who does not love his brother whom he has seen, how can he love God whom he has not seen? And this commandment we have from Him: that he who loves God must love his brother also.*

The Apostle John used strong language when he said that those who say they love God but hate their brother are liars. It was this same apostle who also revealed that God is love and that as His child, that you are to imitate God (1 John 4:8).

Satan is a Deceiver

Satan will use offensive people to come against you. He does this in order to make your love grow cold. When you are ignorant of the way Satan works, you are easily taken advantage of. Second Corinthians 2:11 says, "Lest Satan should take advantage of us; for we are not ignorant of his devices." Consequently, it's vitally important to realize that Satan is a deceiver. He is a spiritual con artist.

In Genesis chapter 3, the serpent spoke with Eve in the Garden of Eden. He tried to convince Eve that what was actually genuine was counterfeit and that what was counterfeit was genuine. The devil will always try to make what is good appear bad and make what is bad appear to be good. He tries to confuse you by twisting the truth so that you won't do what God says. And if you don't do what God says, then you won't receive the blessings that God has promised you.

One way the devil confuses you and twists your thinking is in the area of offense. When an offense comes, you must make a decision, and you will decide to either hold onto the offense or release it. Regardless of whether you make this decision consciously or subconsciously, nonetheless the decision will be made, and you will be the one who makes it.

Embracing offense is so easy, but once it has been embraced, it is almost impossible to get rid of by your own strength and ability. Taking hold of an offense is like reaching out and grabbing a high-voltage electrical wire. Once you grab it, all the electricity going through the cable affects the nerves in your arm and your hand and you cannot let go. Your mind is thinking, *Let go.* Your body is trying to release it, but your hand cannot let go because the nerves in your hand are clutched around the cable. You need help to let go.

Like your hand that is clasped around a high voltage wire, in your own power and strength you cannot release offense. Yet, if you make the decision to get free by faith, and then ask the Lord to help you, God will empower you to release offense and live totally free. The very thing that looks impossible will become a reality when the power of God works through you.

Freedom from offense and hurt can take place as soon as you release it. If you're a born-again believer, God will empower you to do the impossible. Jesus said in

Mark 9:23, "All things are possible to him that believes." When you believe by faith that you can allow offense to go, you will get free and sleep at night like you haven't slept in years.

There is nothing like the peace of God and the rest of God that comes from being free from hurt and offense. This is the peace that Jesus spoke of in John 14:27, "Peace I leave with you, My peace I give to you; not as the world gives do I give to you. Let not your heart be troubled, neither let it be afraid." The world doesn't have the peace that Jesus offers. In fact, nobody can give you peace like the peace Jesus gives you when you obey His Word. And what does the Word tell you to do when you are hurt and offended? Forgive.

How Often Should You Forgive?

Have you ever wondered how much is enough? After all, how much should one person have to put up with? In Matthew 18:21-22, Jesus teaches just how often we should forgive those who offend us. It says,

> Then Peter came to Him and said, 'Lord, how often shall my brother sin against me, and I forgive him? Up to seven times?' Jesus said to him, 'I do not say to you, up to seven times, but up to seventy times seven.'

Seventy times seven was a Jewish idiom that meant there is no limit to the amount of times you must forgive. In today's vernacular that would be equivalent to us saying, "Forgive them a million times if that's what it takes." Jesus indicated that we should not focus on how many times we forgive, but what's important is that we release offense and walk away every time. The consequences of holding onto unforgiveness are simply not worth it.

The world is concerned with behavior modification, but the Word of God teaches about change. The Word doesn't talk about covering up your problems; instead, it talks about eliminating them. Do you know that you don't have to go to a three, six, or twelve-step program? Instead, you can be delivered in a one-step program. I am not criticizing any program that helps people. I simply know God's deliverance is quick, complete, long-lasting, and permanent.

Choose to be Inoffensive

Even though you try not to offend others, it is inevitable that you will offend someone because we are all different, and we don't respond the same way. For example, after preaching, I have had one person say my sermon was the best message they have ever heard, while someone else said I messed up. Two people sat side-by-side and heard the same words, but came away with totally different opinions.

The same differences can occur in a home. Two children can be raised in the same environment. One is a wonderful child, not causing any problems, while the other child is constant trouble. Is it the parents' fault? No, it simply illustrates that everyone hears differently and makes different choices.

However, just because people receive differently, doesn't give you a license to be offensive. No, you must make every effort to be inoffensive. Ephesians 4:32 says, "Be kind to one another, tenderhearted, forgiving one another, just as God in Christ forgave you."

Proverbs 15:1 says, "A soft answer turns away wrath, but a harsh word stirs up anger." This doesn't imply that you are to speak with a quiet voice. No, that's not what it's talking about. Instead, it means to avoid abrasive, harsh speech.

The person endeavoring to be inoffensive won't stir up strife. That means you won't be a talebearer, a tongue-wagger, or a person who cannot wait to spread a bit of juicy information. Instead, you must make the decision to shun strife and offense. Galatians 5:15 says, "But if you bite and devour one another, beware, lest you be consumed by one another. I say then, walk in the Spirit, and you shall not fulfill the lusts of the flesh."

However, no matter how sterling your words are, or how perfect you try to live your life, you cannot control how others react to what you say or do. Many times when Jesus spoke the truth, it offended people. Luke 4:28-29 records the account when Jesus' words made the people so angry that they tried to push Him over a cliff. Even though Jesus didn't say or do anything wrong, the people became angry and offended with Him anyway.

Hurting People Hurt Others

It has been said, "Hurting people hurt people." It means that when someone is offensive and hurtful toward you, you can be assured that it's because they have been hurt. Knowing that it is hurting people who hurt others can actually help you to forgive them.

The same compassion of God that came upon Jesus towards those who crucified Him can envelop you towards those who have hurt you. Luke 23:34 records what Jesus said, "Father, forgive them, for they do not know what they do." The compassion of God can cause you to see that person from a completely different perspective—from God's point of view.

Jesus spoke about this kind of compassion in the parable of the king who decided to settle his accounts. When one of his debtors could not pay his debt, the Word says, "Then the master of that servant was moved with compassion, released him, and forgave him the debt" (Matthew 18:27). This parable is a representation of what Jesus has done for you and me.

First Peter 3:18 says, "For Christ also suffered once for sins, the just for the unjust, that He might bring us to God, being put to death in the flesh but made alive by the Spirit." Jesus, the sinless Son of God, paid the debt for our transgressions when we were totally incapable of doing so. Not only did he pay for our sin, but he bore our sickness and carried our disease so that we could be healed. He exchanged a garment of praise for the spirit of heaviness, and He has turned our mourning into joy.

Consistent with His giving nature, Jesus gave us His anointing to preach the gospel and gave us authority over the devil. He has sent us to heal the brokenhearted, to proclaim liberty to the captives, recovery of sight to the blind, and announce that this is the day when God's free favors profusely abound!

You and I have not come close to suffering what Jesus did, and He did it while we were still hostile toward Him. The pain that offense has caused us—as great as it might be—does not compare to the suffering that Jesus bore for our freedom. Freely we have received, and freely we must give (Matthew 10:8).

There is no offense or hurt that the blood of Jesus cannot cleanse. Not one thing that you have experienced is too great for the blood of Jesus. Speak this confession today and set in motion the supernatural power of God on your behalf.

My Confession of Deliverance

❑ I <u>release</u> all hurts and offenses of the past and present.

❑ I commit to <u>renew</u> my mind daily with the Word of God.

❑ I <u>resolve</u> to seek Christian fellowship in a Bible based church.

❑ I <u>refuse</u> to allow offenses to attach themselves to me.

❑ I <u>rejoice</u> in my freedom.

❑ I claim my <u>reward</u> of peace.

The Lord will empower you to do the impossible. Receive God's supernatural empowerment to forgive and begin your journey of offense-free living!

How to Become a Christian

There is only one way to have everlasting life. There is only one way to live forever and be assured that you will always be with the Lord. There is only one way to the kingdom of God and the kingdom of heaven. There is only one way to the Father, and that one way is Jesus.

God loved you so much that He sent Jesus to earth to pay the price for your sins and make a way for you to live forever with Him. He paid the price you could not pay. He made a way of escape from the bondage of sin and death.

Receiving the gift of salvation is simple. It basically involves five steps. Read these steps and the Scriptures. Then pray and accept the gift of salvation.

Step #1 You Must Believe in Jesus

"For God so loved the world that He gave His only begotten Son, that whoever believes in Him should not perish but have everlasting life. For God did not send His Son into the world to condemn the world, but that the world through Him might be saved" (John 3:16-17).

"Believe on the Lord Jesus Christ, and you will be saved, you and your household" (Acts 16:31).

Step #2 You Must Confess Your Sins

You must acknowledge that you are a sinner, and you want Jesus to wash your sins away.

"If we confess our sins, He is faithful and just to forgive us our sins and to cleanse us from all unrighteousness" (1 John 1:9).

Step #3 You Must Repent *(Turn away from your sins)*

"For the wages of sin is death, but the gift of God is eternal life in Christ Jesus our Lord" (Romans 6:23).

"The time is fulfilled, and the kingdom of God is at hand. Repent and believe in the gospel" (Mark 1:15).

Step #4 You Must Confess Jesus Before Men

"If you <u>confess with your mouth</u> the Lord Jesus and <u>believe in your heart</u> that God has raised Him from the dead, you will be saved. For with the heart one believes unto righteousness, and with the mouth confession is made unto salvation" (Romans 10:9-10).

Step #5 You Must Accept the Gift of Salvation

"For by grace you have been saved through faith, and that not of yourselves; it is the gift of God" (Ephesians 2:8).

"But as many as received Him, to them He gave the right to become children of God, to those who believe in His name" (John 1:12).

"Behold, now is the accepted time; behold, now is the day of salvation "(2 Corinthians 6:2).

Dear Heavenly Father,

I come in the name of Jesus. I thank you for sending your Son, Jesus, into this world to die and for raising Him from the dead so that I can have everlasting life.

I recognize Jesus as my Savior and as the Lord of my life. I repent of my sins, and I forgive those who have wronged me. I believe in my heart, and I will confess openly my belief in Jesus. Thank you for forgiving me of my sins and giving me eternal life.

I receive this gift by faith,

In Jesus' name, Amen.

"I say to you that likewise there will be more joy in heaven over one sinner who repents than over ninety-nine just persons who need no repentance." -Jesus

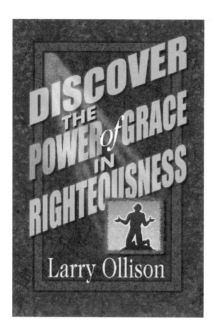

Discover the Power of Grace in Righteousness

You have probably heard grace defined as God's unmerited favor and that is absolutely true, but it is so much more. In our own strength and abilities we can sometimes do the possible, but God's grace empowers the Christian to do the impossible. Truly, it seems God always calls us to do the impossible—but with His grace working in our lives, the impossible becomes reality.

LARRY OLLISON

God's Plan for Handling Stress

Many people live under continual stress. Stress from work, finances, health, family, and even stress from religion has destroyed many lives. This does not have to be.

There are two plans for your life. God has a plan and the Prince of Darkness has a plan. The choice is yours. Satan's plan will create confusion, fear, and worry. It will eventually lead to total destruction. God's plan will eliminate stress and produce peace. God's plan is FAITH. Only through faith can peace be obtained.

Is Faith Really Important?

Health and prosperity should be the standard lifestyle of a Christian. However, many attend church, pray, and sincerely seek God for help, and still live below God's best.

Why would a Christian who asks God for healing and financial help not receive it? Well, the answer is so simple that it's often overlooked. Without this one key, the Word of God will not profit you. Discover the catalyst that will activate the Word of God in your life and set you free from the bondage of sickness and poverty.

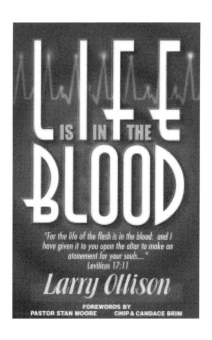

Life is in the Blood

Can a believer really defeat the devil? Is it possible to live free from the fears and worries of this world? Dr. Larry Ollison answers these questions with a resounding, "Yes!"

Leviticus 17:11 says, "For the life of the flesh is in the blood...." Larry takes you step by step, scripture by scripture into such a revelation of faith that even a young child can learn how to live the Christian life in victory.

This book provides every tool you need to confidently walk out the promises of God. You will never be afraid to stand nose to nose with the devil again. It is a must for any believer who wants to walk in the fullness of God's provision.

ABOUT THE AUTHOR

Dr. Larry Ollison was raised a Southern Baptist. He majored in theology at Southwest Baptist University and received his Ph.D. from Life Christian University.

Larry is the author of several books and articles and his weekly newspaper column is widely read.

Larry is a Director for *International Convention of Faith Ministries* and Vice President of *Spirit FM Christian Radio Network*. He is also the host of *The Cutting Edge* radio broadcast and authors *The Cutting Edge Daily Devotional,* featured daily on CFAITH.com.

Larry is the founder of Bibles Behind Bars prison ministry and TIPI Ministries (an outreach ministry to Native Americans).

Larry is Senior Pastor of *Walk on the Water Faith Church,* Founder and President of *Faith Bible Training Center,* a member of *Who's Who Worldwide,* and on the board of several corporations and international ministries.

Larry is a pastor, pilot, teacher, and author. His number one goal is to meet the needs of the people through the teaching of faith in God's Word.

Larry and his wife, Loretta, have two children, Sherrie and Robbie. Sherrie is a graduate of Oral Roberts University. She lives in Tulsa, OK with her husband, Christopher Kennedy, and their three daughters. Robbie is a graduate of Southwest Missouri State University and lives in Osage Beach, MO, with his wife, Julie, and their two sons.